A New Deal for the Tropics

A New Deal for the Tropics

Puerto Rico during the Depression Era, 1932-1935

MANUEL R. RODRÍGUEZ

Markus Wiener Publishers
Princeton

Copyright © 2010 by Markus Wiener Publishers, Princeton, New Jersey

All rights reserved. No part of this book may be reproduced or transmitted in any form or by any means, whether electronic or mechanical—including photocopying or recording—or through any information storage or retrieval system, without permission of the copyright owners.

For information, write to Markus Wiener Publishers
231 Nassau Street, Princeton, NJ 08542
www.markuswiener.com

Library of Congress Cataloging-in-Publication Data

Rodriguez, Manuel R., 1967-
A new deal for the tropics : Puerto Rico during the Depression era, 1932-1935 / Manuel R. Rodriguez.
    p. cm.
Includes bibliographical references.
ISBN 978-1-55876-517-7 (hardcover : acid-free paper)
ISBN 978-1-55876-518-4 (pbk. : acid-free paper)
1. Puerto Rico—History—1898-1952. 2. Depressions—1929—Puerto Rico. 3. New Deal, 1933-1939—Puerto Rico. I. Puerto Rico Emergency Relief Administration. II. Title.
F1975.R638 2010
338.97295009'043—dc22
                        2010033364

Markus Wiener Publishers books are printed in the United States of America on acid-free paper and meet the guidelines for permanence and durability of the Committee on Production Guidelines for Book Longevity of the Council on Library Resources.

CONTENTS

Acknowledgments vii

Introduction 1
    A New Historiography Approach   4
    Development and Governmentality   7
    About Documentary Sources and Methodology   12
    Chapter Overvier   15

CHAPTER 1
Bringing the Promise of Modernity: A New Deal for Puerto Rico, 1932-1935 21
    The Arrival of the Depression in Puerto Rico, 1929-1933   21
    The Political Landscape   25
    The Quest for a Colonial Relationship   28
    The New Deal in Puerto Rico   31

CHAPTER 2
From Emergency Relief to Development: The Emergence of the Puerto Rico Emergency Relief Administration 45
    The PRERA as a Development Project   45
    The Politics of Representation   47
    The Bureaucracy of Development   55

CHAPTER 3
The Heralds of Modernity: The Role of Puerto Rican Professionals in the Puerto Rican Relief Administration 67
    Professionalization and the Institutionalization of the PRERA   67
    The Construction of an Integral Bureaucrat   70
    Technical Expertise, Efficiency, Progress, and Modernity   76
    Strategies of Deployment: The PRERA as a Nationalist Discourse   81

CHAPTER 4
The Deployment of Development: The Implementation of the PRERA Programs and Their Impact on Puerto Rican Society 93

    Making the New Deal Attractive to the Population   93
    The PRERA Programs in the Daily Lives of Puerto Ricans   94
    Rethinking the Presence of the U.S. Government:
        The Subaltern Perceptions about the Development
        Policies of the Roosevelt Administration   107

CHAPTER 5
The Limits of the PRERA as a Development Project and the Rise of a New Government Rationale 125

    The Collapse of the PRERA as a Development Initiative   125
    The Puerto Rico Reconstruction Administration as a
        Continuation of the PRERA   128
    Beyond the Collapse: The Art of Governance as a
        Biopolitical Strategy   138

Conclusion 147

Appendix: Illustrations 153

Bibliography 155

ACKNOWLEDGMENTS

During the almost four years that it took me to write this book, I have reaffirmed the fact that the completion of a book is a process that involves the collective efforts of many people. I am grateful for the intellectual insights and continuous support of my professors at Temple University—Dr. Kenneth Kusmer, Dr. Richard Immerman, Dr. Phil Evanson, Dr. Wilbert Jenkins, and Dr. Robert Schoewel—and my advisor, Dr. Arthur Schmidt. I want to express my sincerest gratitude to Dr. Schmidt. His availability at all times despite his many academic obligations, his constant caring about and advice for my professional career during all these years, his recommendations as to how to enrich this text, and his friendship and kindness are greatly appreciated. I also want to thank the Future Faculty Fellowship program of Temple University. Their financial support and concern during my graduate student years made possible the research for this project.

I am also in debt to my colleagues in the Department of History at the University of Puerto Rico and at other academic institutions in the United States: Carlos Pabón, Pedro San Miguel, Fernando Picó, Javier Figueroa, Jorge Lizardi, Carlos D. Altagracia, Gabriel Villaronga, Mayra Rosario, Gonzalo Córdova, Ivette Sepúlveda, José "Cheo" O. Solá, Víctor Vázquez, Gilbert Joseph, Stuart Schwartz, María Jordán, Aldo Lauria and Félix Matos. I want to express my deepest gratitude to Carlos, Pedro, Aldo, and Cheo for all the years of encouragement in my moments of doubt, challenging me intellectually and quickly responding to my apprehensions about the writing of this book. Their insights and suggestions greatly enriched the academic quality of this text. I am also grateful for the support of a circle of important people who have been with me since I started this academic project: Alfredo Torres, Armando Cruz, Cezanne Cardona, Juan Negrón Ayala, Héctor Freire, Javier Ortiz, Antonio Hernández, and Meghan Shelby. Thanks for your continuous friendship and support. I want to express my gratitude to my friend of many years, Marién Hernández, who, despite short notice, made time to create the artwork on the cover of this book. I also want to recognize the efforts of my editor, Adam Juchniewicz, who corrected the manuscript.

The academic content of this project would not have been possible without the help of the people who are in charge of preserving the sources necessary for its completion. I want to recognize the professionalism demonstrated by the personnel at the Franklin D. Roosevelt Library at Hyde Park, the National Archives in Washington DC, and the Center of Historical Research of the Department of History at the University of Puerto Rico. I am particularly grateful to the staff of the Puerto Rican Collection at the Library José Lázaro of the University of Puerto Rico for providing me with photographs for the cover of this book from their Puerto Rico Reconstruction Administration collection. Special thanks to the staff of the Puerto Rico General Archives at San Juan, Puerto Rico—especially to Milagros Pepín and José (Cheo) Pérez. Their expertise, excellent service, professionalism, and love for cigars made the tedious hours of research an unforgettable memory.

I also want to recognize the continuous love and support of my family. My father, Cruz M. Rodríguez; my mother, Carmen E. Vázquez de Rodríguez; my brother, Ricardo A. Rodríguez; my sister-in-law, María Rosa Martí; my *compañera*, Arlene Marrero; and my daughter, Camila Ariana. I cannot imagine having got to this point without their example, their love, and their continuous support. They all inspired me to overcome the obstacles that I have encountered throughout this journey.

Finally, this book is dedicated to the memory of my beloved grandfather, Ramón Vázquez. His passion for seeking knowledge inspired me to pursue an academic career. Without his love and example, I probably would not be writing these words.

INTRODUCTION

The September 21, 1935 editorial page of *La Rehabilitación,* the official newspaper of the Puerto Rico Emergency Relief Administration (PRERA), provided an image that transcended the function of the typical New Deal relief agency:

> "It is unquestionable that the effects produced by the PRERA in the social lives and economic structures of Puerto Rico were invaluable. Today we can see that any movement in agriculture, commerce and industry is due to the positive intervention of the PRERA. Roads have been built, buildings have been constructed and training has been provided to citizens of both sexes to improve their opportunities to get a job. New incentives in the industrial field have opened a market for native products for the purpose of revitalizing the island's economy. In agricultural activities the PRERA has shown to be a superb initiative. It has created farms, distributed seed, taught modern methods of agriculture, and provided technical orientation to small-farm peasants in order to industrialize its production. In the field of education, the PRERA has provided work to hundreds of teachers, making possible the education of thousands of children. Synthesizing all these facts, the PRERA has been a blessing to this island improving its economy and providing thousands of families with bread and clothing and monetary aid for the payments of housing rent, and in countless other cases procuring help to many displaced people that was called to its doors."[1]

At first glance, this description of the activities of the PRERA in Puerto Rico is similar to the ones sponsored by the Federal Emergency Administration programs scattered throughout the United States in the early 1930s. For the first time in United States and Puerto Rico history, the federal government assumed a prominent role in the lives of its citizens by providing welfare relief and work for the unemployed and regulated corporate capital. Like most countries in the world, Puerto Rico received the full impact of the collapse of the stock market in 1929. Wages afterwards reached their lowest level since the U.S. invasion in 1898. The sugar industry, the main economic industry on the island, had to limit its production as a result of the 1932 Agricultural Adjustment Administration (AAA), and thousands of workers lost their jobs.[2] In the meantime, political unrest started to emerge throughout the island. Under the leadership of Dr. Pedro Albizu Campos, the Nationalist Party demanded the independence of Puerto Rico from the United States. According to Albizu Campos, the Treaty of Paris which ended the Spanish-American-Cuban War, and had transferred the island from Spain to the United States was illegal because it lacked the consent of Puerto Ricans. As a result, the nationalists were reluctant to recognize the presence of U.S. institutions on the island, sparking a period of violence during the 1930s that culminated with the arrest of several Nationalist Party leaders, including Albizu Campos.

Certainly, the hectic events of the early 1930s had complex origins beyond either the economic havoc caused by the Depression or the political instability that questioned U.S. rule on the island. These events reflected the deterioration and fragility of the political relationship established in 1898 between the United States and Puerto Rico. The Great Depression was the catalyst that ignited this crisis. In its wake, federal government agencies, intellectuals, and some members of the local political elite realized that a new political consensus was necessary to preserve the colonial establishment. The New Deal and the PRERA provided a common ground to establish such a solution.

The programs sponsored by the New Deal provided the presence of the United States in Puerto Rico with a new and benevolent face, one concerned with improving the well-being of its colonial subjects through the PRERA initiatives. Many sectors of the population stricken by the Depression saw in the PRERA a valuable opportunity to improve their material conditions after three decades of "colonial negligence." More than a distant entity, the United States government became an agent that permeated the daily lives of Puerto Ricans. This change of perception laid the foundations for the realignment of political governance in Puerto Rico during the 1930s. This understanding was based on the tolerance of the United States presence on the island, in a time of crisis and the further preservation of a colonial regime that would last until the present day.

These actions have raised questions that I intend to answer through this book. Why did the political elite and the New Dealers create an image of the PRERA as a development project, able to transform the economic and social conditions of Puerto Rico? In what ways did the local population perceive and integrate the PRERA programs into its daily life? How did the PRERA contribute to establishing a consensus among the metropolitan state (the United States), the local bureaucracy, and subaltern members of the population to preserve and transform the colonial relationship between the United States and Puerto Rico? Did the PRERA contribute to governmentalize the colonial rule in Puerto Rico established in 1898? The purpose of this book is to examine the implementation of the New Deal's PRERA. It was conceived and implemented as a modernizing development project during the 1930s. While traditional U.S and Puerto Rican historiography have explained that the PRERA as a simple and short-lived New Deal agency simply limited to the distribution of massive emergency relief aid among the needy population built upon the idea that far from of being another New Deal's welfare agency, the PRERA implemented a complex development project that governmentalized the American colonial rule in the island in the early 1930s. Such progress transformed the role of the government and the way in which it exercises power, throughout the regulation of the biological aspects of the population. Based on this argument, I will focus on the PRERA as a complex development project carefully crafted through a discourse of progress and modernity that aimed to transform in the long term the colonial relationship between United States and Puerto Rico. I believe that this development discourse and its impact on the population's cultural practices of Puerto Rico significantly contributed to shaping the vision of the colonial subjects to the metropolitan authorities and brought forth a new series of strategies for political, social, and cultural domination that ultimately led to the establishment of a new rational of government by the early 1930s. This new rational was focus on a redefinition of the US government on the island more oriented to guarantee the well-being of its population through the establishment of an extended array of developmental initiatives brought forth by the PRERA.

A New Historiography Approach

Traditional historiography has overlooked the perspective that I frame in this study. Scholarly works about the presence of the New Deal in territorial possessions have been scarce. Puerto Rican and American historiography have limited the New Deal initiatives to welfare programs that ended in failure because of either political controversies among local political parties or excessive micro-management from Washington D. C. In some cases, as happened with the United States historiography, the extension of the New Deal policies to territorial possessions has been constantly overlooked. During the late 1940s and 1950s, the Consensus School offered one of the first explanations of the presence of the New Deal in the United States. The post-war years represented for many historians the logical outcome from a century of consolidation of the liberal, democratic, and progressive virtues of the United States. From the chaotic years of the Great Depression and the ashes from World War II, a political, social, and even economic "consensus" emerged as an element that consolidated those virtues. Scholars such as James McGregor Burns, Richard Hofstadter, and Arthur M. Schlesinger Jr. are among the most well-know scholars who subscribe to this approach towards the studies of the New Deal.[3]

The interpretative efforts of the Consensus school articulate an image of the New Deal as the triumph of the U.S. capitalist system and institutions. However, most Consensus scholars overlook the fact that the New Deal did not provide the blessings of American exceptionalism to other sectors of U.S. society, such as to ethnic groups or to those living in territorial possessions such as Puerto Rico.

During the 1960s, the New Left School emerged as the most important interpretive effort for the study of the New Deal. Its most important approach centered on the concept of Corporate Liberalism utilized by historians Barton Bernstein, Ronald Radosh, Ellis Hawley, Robert Wiebe, Kim McQuaid, Robert Cuff, Robert Collins, Fred Block and Louis Galambos.[4] The Corporate Liberalism theory argues that New

Deal policies, such as Social Security and the National Recovery Administration, were the result of a consensus between corporate capital and the state that would in the end, benefit both partners in the achievement of their particular interests. Other historians have focused on the New Deal from other perspectives. These scholars have chosen other political models to explain the presence of the New Deal beyond the constraints of the Corporate Liberalism model and its technocratic orientation. Topics such as state, gender, ecology, labor, the emergence of a welfare state, ethnicity and citizenship were all the prime subjects of their scholarly efforts.[5]

Some studies within U.S. historiography focus on the implementation of the New Deal in Puerto Rico. The most representative study of the New Deal presence in Puerto Rico has been written by Thomas Mathews in the 1960s.[6] The book concentrates mainly on the impact of New Deal policies upon local politics. Mathews provides a general description of the political changes in the United States and the island by the early 1930s, a scenario for the political conflict that permeated the entire decade. The implementation of the PRERA and the Puerto Rico Reconstruction Administration (PRRA) constitute the core of his analysis. Mathews vividly describes how local political organizations struggled to assume control of the federal funds in both programs. The result was that Puerto Rican political organizations used the Roosevelt reforms to further their own partisan interests.

Other English-language works, such as one written by historian Gordon Lewis, follow Mathews regarding the limited effects of the New Deal in Puerto Rico and its eventual failure to cope with the problems on the island.[7] Lewis agrees with Mathews in that the New Deal ended the "imperialism of neglect" enforced by the United States after thirty-two years of colonial domination. Lewis sustains that the application of New Deal programs, such as the FERA, the NRA, the AAA, and later the reconstruction plans envisioned by the PRRA, constituted a valuable opportunity to deal with the socio-economic problems brought by the Depression. But, according to Lewis's analysis, "the New Deal dies in Puerto Rico in 1940 as surely as it died in the continental United States".[8] Although Lewis accepts the failure of the New Deal on the island, his analysis differs from that of Mathews. For Lewis, the causes of the New Deal's failure were not exclusively political. His analysis focuses more on the structural conception of the New Deal and its potential to change the colonial relationship between the United States and Puerto Rico.

Lewis pointed out that the lack of a rational and efficient administrative unit to regulate colonial affairs in Puerto Rico doomed the New Deal effectiveness. As the author suggests, "the absence of an ideological commitment to the empire naturally entailed, in its wake, the absence of any sustained effort to build up any sort of special and permanent machinery for the government of the new empire".[9] In summary, Lewis suggests that the United States failed in its responsibility to provide the bureaucratic institutions needed for the administration and welfare for its Caribbean possession.

Traditionally, the New Deal occupies a small role in Puerto Rican scholarship. For scholars engaged in the study of the 1930s in Puerto Rico, the image of the Depression, based on either the collapse of the stock market in 1929 or the long lines in the city to receive government hand outs did not represent an abrupt change with the past. These were elements experienced by Puerto Ricans even before the collapse of the stock market. Puerto Rican historiography instead focuses on the events of the 1930s as a period in which diverse sectors of Puerto Rican society started to question U.S. colonial domination over the island, a time in which the metropolitan state attempted to implement some aspects of the New Deal reforms while, in the midst of a re-emergence for a national identity.[10] Notwithstanding, the New Deal has been regarded as a secondary actor in the context of the economically and socially chaotic times of the Great Depression. For some scholars such as Fernando Picó, Francisco Scarano, María D. Luque, and Blanca Silvestrini, the PRERA was considered as another emergency agency of the Roosevelt administration.[11] For others such as Emilio González, Ángel Quintero Rivera, Emilio Pantojas, Leonardo Santana Rabell, and Nilsa Burgos, the New Deal in Puerto Rico was presented as the direct predecessor of the populist development projects established in the island by the Popular Democratic Party during the 1940s. Other scholars and intellectual think tanks such as Blanca Silvestrini, Cesar Rey and Taller de Formación Política have devoted their efforts to offers a particular view of the New Deal and its impact upon the Puerto Rican working class during the 1930s and 1940s.[12]

All of these reports have studied the presence of the New Deal from various angles, contributing to a better understanding of the program's intention in Puerto Rico during the 1930s. However, this scholarship has underestimated the presence of the PRERA in Puerto Rico as a New Deal agency, therefore limiting its true impact and importance to a mere welfare agency that alienated local politics. This book wants to present an alternative analysis about the presence of the PRERA in Puerto Rico in two areas which have never been considered before in devotion to this topic: first, studying the PRERA, as the first New Deal agency established on the island rather than as the predecessor of the PRRA, and secondly analyzing the PRERA as an ambitious development project that penetrated multiple aspects of Puerto Rican society, which over the long term re-articulated the colonial relationship between the United States and Puerto Rico.

The analysis presented throughout this study is not interested in following methodological or analytical patterns similar to the ones discussed above. I will avoid any analysis regarding the New Deal as a welfare agency that failed as a result of the lack of funding and the inefficiency of the bureaucratic structure which supported it. I will also avoid mentioning the other traditional perspectives, such as the endless controversies caused by the New Deal in the realm of insular politics, or if its programs were a strategy of imperial domination.[13] It is in this context in which I want to approach the PRERA from theoretical perspective that emphasizes the conception of this New Deal initiative as a development project.

Development and Governmentality

During the 1990s, the concept of development had been studied as a powerful discourse on political domination in so-called "third-world" countries. Amongst the works regarding this topic is a study by anthropologist James Ferguson. Ferguson focuses on the impact of development, depoliticization and bureaucratic power in the African country of Lesotho.[14] Ferguson offers a detailed study about how the application of different developmental projects in Lesotho did not constitute a strategy to eradicate poverty but constituted a "machine" in which the state exercises bureaucratic power over the subjects. The promises of modernity and progress made by the developmental offensive were used by the state to depoliticize sectors of the population that might have been opposed to such projects. Development was portrayed by developed countries as the panacea that would end the economic and social misery, providing a custom solution which had to be accepted by the people of the country. This process of integration and acceptance of the development project had the effect that vast portion of the population no longer depending anymore on the process of political negotiation.

Anthropologist Stacy L. Pigg conducted another important study about the development of the third world in Nepal. Pigg argues that the developmental projects implemented in Nepal during the post-colonial period were not measures unilaterally imposed by the former colonial state or local power elite. Instead, local populations accepted modernity and combined it with local cultural practices. Development, according to the author, has to be seen as a hybrid process that fuses the local with the global societies to which it is applied. Pigg concentrates her efforts amongst how the modern discourse of development is represented on the rural population of Nepal and in what ways it is integrated into everyday practices. Accordingly, Pigg analyzes how development has contributed to forging a national community and how the education system has encouraged the Nepalese peasantry to articulate the premises of modernity to their villages. The ideology of modernization embodied in these development programs, instead of an imposition, constitutes for Pigg a social map that "serves as a guide in orienting people in all sectors of Nepalese society."[15]

The study of development as a discourse of political domination and consensus has also been applied to the particular case of Latin America. The work of anthropologist Arturo Escobar emphasizes the study of development within this new approach. Escobar focuses on how the different projects of development implemented in Colombia during the early 1970s ended in failure. Throughout his study, Escobar provides a detailed analysis that explains the collapse of the development projects in this South American country.[16] According to Escobar, after World War II, first-world countries envisioned an era of prosperity that would guarantee stability and economic development on a global basis. In order to guarantee the success of such a project, it was necessary to create a discourse capable of convincing other countries of the potential benefits embodied within it. This developmental discourse would embody the promises of progress and modernization to the countries that participated in the developmental initiatives proposed by the first-world countries. As a result and because of the economic reorientation of the world economy during the post-war years, many of the so-called third-world countries accepted the imposed category of under-developed seeking a solution to their national economic and social problems. Such acceptance of this "underdevelopment" condition paved the way for the introduction of new knowledge and other aspects that characterized modernity: new agricultural technology, the construction of infrastructure, and the professionalization and creation of a technocracy able to reproduce and implement such knowledge. As a result, the first-world countries created a "representation" of the third world as an incapable entity unable to implement creative solutions to its own problems without the intervention of foreign countries.

This regime of representation is constituted in another invention of the West to analyze, dissect, understand, exercise power, and impose their parameters of progress over the "other." The impact of development as representation constitutes the crux of Escobar's argument, and it has been used as an "extremely efficient apparatus for producing knowledge about, and in the exercise of power over third world countries."[17] The regime of representation has the purpose of exercising political domination throughout the creation of a discourse that establishes that development equals progress "places of encounter were identities are constructed."[18] One of the byproducts of such a process is the articulation of consensus between those that want to impose development and the beneficiaries of that developmental order.

The implementation of the PRERA in Puerto Rico tends to illustrate this process. In order to guarantee the success of New Deal programs such as the PRERA, the United States government had to create a developmental project in Puerto Rico in which the implementation of modern and progressive developmental initiatives came to the "rescue" of the natives, in order to save them from the deplorable situation in which they were trapped. The crisis brought on by the Depression and the rapid deterioration of the colonial system that bound the island to the United States since 1898 offered the perfect historic juncture for the realization of such a project. The educational programs, the newly agricultural techniques, the imposition of a hygiene discourse, the emergence of a technocratic bureaucracy and its professionalization reflected an image of progress, a compromise with modernity for the betterment of society based on the modern and scientific discourses imposed by the United States in Puerto Rico.[19] At the same time, U.S. colonial authorities, with the close cooperation of local political and intellectual interests, utilized the discourse of progress and modernity, brought by the PRERA programs, to normalize and control Puerto Ricans, making them colonial subjects more receptive to domination. At the same time, a consensus emerged between New Dealers (colonial authorities), local power elite and subalterns that guaranteed political stability and the preservation of the colonial order established in 1898. During this process the subaltern was an inert body subjected to the domination of these elite. They formed new strategies of negotiation and legitimization of the existing political order throughout the integration of the developmental initiatives of the PRERA. For instance, peasants accepted the programs of the agricultural cooperatives in order to improve the capitalization of their products and participated in educational programs and vocational programs for social advancement. The development programs implemented by the PRERA significantly contributed to creating a social imaginary in which the United States transformed itself from a distant metropolis to a governmental entity concerned with the well being of the population.

One of the most important effects of the development initiatives brought by the PRERA was the governmentalization of the United States presence in Puerto Rico. In order to understand this process, it is important to understand the theoretical proposals of Michel Foucault about the transformation of the rational of government. Foucault criticizes the overuse of the concept of the State suggesting that it has to be decentralized as the only manifestation of institutional power. "The State is no more than a composite reality and a mythized abstraction, whose importance is a more lot limited than many of us think. Maybe what is more important to our modernity –that is for our present- is not much the *etatisation* of society as the *governmentalization* of the State".[20] Based on this analysis Foucault suggests that the transformation of government since the eighteenth century and not the State became the priority in the study of how power is exercised upon the population. Accordingly, he announces the emergence of a new era of governmentality by saying:

> "the ensemble formed by the institutions, procedures, analysis and reflections, the calculations and tactics that allow the exercise of this very specific albeit complex form of power, which has as its target population, as its principal form of knowledge political economy, and as its essential technical means apparatuses of security, the tendency which, over a long period and throughout the West, has steadily led towards the pre-eminence over all other forms (sovereignty, discipline, etc.) of this type of power which may be termed government, resulting, on the one hand, in the formation of a whole series of specific governmental apparatuses, and on the other, in the development of a whole complex of *saviors*."[21]

What Foucault is proposing is a new perspective to understand what government is in the modern age. He argues that starting in the eighteenth century; the concept of government experienced a profound transformation from an institution whose power emanated from juridical sovereignty to an institution more concerned with the regulation of populations. As Colin Gordon argues, the term "government" became a practice aiming to shape, guide or affect the conduct of some person or persons, that involves the studies of who can govern, what governing is and who is governed.[22] As a result of this reorientation of priorities, the population became the reason of the government, in the instance in which exercises power. As Foucault points out:

> "Population comes to appear above all else as the ultimate end of government. In contrast to sovereignty, government has its purpose not the act of government itself, but the welfare of the population, the improvement of its condition, the increase of its wealth, longetivity, health etc."[23]

Population then became the priority of the modern government.

Government efforts were directed to regulate the population, potentiate life and let live[24]. Foucault calls this process biopower or biopolitics. Throughout biopolitics the government is going to exercise power throughout the monitoring and control of the biological processes, populations' growth, public health, life expectancy, housing, economic observations, and migration. The government reserves for itself the regulations of these problems in a concept called by Foucault, the "biopolitics of the population".[25] Throughout this biopolitical management the government will concentrate its efforts in the "administration of the bodies and the calculation of life" and the development of numerous and diverse techniques to obtain the subjection of the bodies and the control of the populations.[26]

It is my contention that the development programs brought by the PRERA governmentalized the colonial rule of the United States in Puerto Rico in the early 1930s. The PRERA reshaped the traditional ways in which the United States exercised power in Puerto Rico. The regulation of the biological aspects of the population and its well being became a new technology of power that soon transformed the political relations between the two countries until the present day. This book aims to explore in detail this process.

About Documentary Sources and Methodology

The location of documentary sources for the study of the PRERA in Puerto Rico has represented one of the most important challenges for the completion of this project because of their scattered distribution on the East coast of the United States and Puerto Rico. The few studies dealing about the presence of the New Deal in Puerto Rico have limited themselves to using the National Archives in Washington D.C., the Franklin D. Roosevelt Library in Hyde Park, New York, as well as to the information acquired from Puerto Rican newspapers published in the early 1930s. These documentary sources have been used mainly to study the impact of the New Deal in local Puerto Rican politics and the emergence of PRRA as an extension of the New Deal policy on the island.

One of the goals of this book is to explore the possibilities of these documentary collections using the PRERA as a point of departure to provide an alternative to the conventional studies of the New Deal in Puerto Rico. Accordingly, one of the first documentary collections studied in this project were Record Groups 350 and 126 located in the Washington Archives at Washington D.C. These Record Groups cover the period from 1898 to 1952, containing documentation concerning social, political, economic, and bureaucratic issues between the United States and Puerto Rico.[27] I consider the materials found in this collection important to recreate the initial years of the New Deal in Puerto Rico. Throughout its letter collection, both Record Groups offer interesting insight about the point of views, decisions, obstacles and personal opinions of New Dealers and local officials concerning the implementation of the initial New Deal programs on the island. In the process of reviewing these sources, I realized that the controversies generated by the New Deal policies on the island transcended the realm of local politics. These sources reflected the resistance of conservative groups to the New Deal and the effort made by the state to penetrate an institutional realm that traditionally belonged to the local political establishment.

The Franklin D. Roosevelt Library at Hyde Park, New York also provided important documentation for the completion of this project, particularly the papers about Harry Hopkins and the Franklin D. Roosevelt Official Papers Appointments. One of the potential shortcomings for the study of the operations of the PRERA in Puerto Rico is the lack of personal archives of key officials who constituted the core of the agency's officials. That is the case of James Bourne, William Font, and Justo Pastor Rivera, important PRERA officials whose documentation was limited to newspapers and public archives.[28] Despite these shortcomings, the documents consulted in the FDR library have been of seminal importance for one of the main goals of this book: to understand the presence of the PRERA in Puerto Rico, not as another New Deal relief agency but as an early blue print of a development project. The papers of Harry Hopkins, Administrator of the PRERA, and the FDR official papers have been important in providing an alternative analysis about this agency in Puerto Rico. This collection provides important documentation that reflects the image and the language used by New Dealers and local officials to portray the PRERA as an "indispensable measure" to save Puerto Rico from economic and social decay. Analyzing the discourse contained in these documents, this book aims to prove that the establishment of the PRERA, far from being a simple relief agency, constituted a well-orchestrated development project.

This study emphasizes new archival sources for the study of the PRERA in Puerto Rico, such as the FERA Central Files (Record Group 69) at Washington D.C., as well as the PRERA Annual Report and the agency's bulletin *La Rehabilitación,* both located in the Library of Congress. The PRERA's organizational structure has not been investigated by any previous study related as to the establishment of the New Deal on the island. The PRERA Annual Report and the FERA Central Files contained in Record Group 69 offered me the unique opportunity of explore the bureaucratic organization and complexities of the PRERA organization and activities in Puerto Rico. The most important documents used in this book have been derived from *La Rehabilitación.* Barely used by previous investigators, this valuable source has provided with important documentation about the daily operations of the agency, its involvement with the public, and the position of the different PRERA officials on the agency's operations. It also has provided a glimpse at the professional profile and modernizing discourses employed by the PRERA's upper echelon of the hierarchy. Previous studies constantly made reference to the "people" who formed the ranks of the PRERA without making any analysis about their particular viewpoint about the complex situation that they faced in the daily operations of the agency.

Puerto Rican collections have been also a source of excellent documentation for the completion of this project. The Fortaleza Collection of the General Archives of Puerto Rico proved to be of great importance for the completion of this project. These documents provided a look at the participation and views of Puerto Ricans concerning the PRERA. The Center for Puerto Rican Studies at Hunter College, New York and the Puerto Rican Collection at the University of Puerto Rico provided sources for this book. The important collection of local newspapers was essential to fill in some gaps in the sometimes scattered documentation of the PRERA. The Annual Governors Reports from 1932 to 1935 located in both archives provided first-hand data, statistics and figures that constituted a great source to contextualize the rapid transformations of local economy in Puerto Rico in the early 1930s. These reports offer a powerful insight to the operations of the local government institutions, as well as the federal programs applied at that time to the island.

Documents and archival material on the PRERA remain scattered in a considerable number of archival institutions in Puerto Rico and the U.S. East coast. To make matters worse, a substantial part of these sources are not filed in an orderly fashion or organized by any topical order. Despite these difficulties, the existing documentary sources regarding the PRERA have allowed me to fulfill the goals of my investigation. In an effort to present an alternative perspective about the PRERA, this book has revised most of the material used by previous works about this topic. This revisionist effort has responded to a four decade tendency of explaining the New Deal and the PRERA presence in Puerto Rico in political terms, leaving behind the complexities of its programs and undermining its impact upon Puerto Rican society. This book aims to fill this weakness and provide a new explanation that will present the PRERA as a development project that re-articulated the power relations in Puerto Rican society and made possible the changes within the political situation between two countries.

Chapter Overview

The introduction will provide an extensive analysis of the traditional historiography of New Deal in the United States and Puerto Rico. It will propose a new historiographical approach based on the PRERA as a developmental project that transformed the political relationship between the United States and Puerto Rico by setting new rational of governmentality. Chapter one will map the different ways in which the Great Depression affected Puerto Rico in the early 1930s and the implementation of the New Deal programs on the island as a response for the crisis. Chapter two will explore the strategies employed in the articulation of a regime of representation committed to deliver a "promise" of modernity and progress capable of transforming the poor material conditions of the island as a result of the effects of the Great Depression. Such changes were indispensable in order to make the different developmental initiatives of the PRERA acceptable to the population. This chapter will also provide a detailed analysis of the PRERA bureaucratic structure, the deployment of the PRERA programs on the island and the elements that contributed to the fruitful completion of such a project. Chapter three will cover the construction of this regime of representation by the American New Dealers and the Puerto Rican professional class appointed to the direction of the PRERA. In order to illustrate this process, this chapter will focus on the discursive strategies that these groups utilized in order to legitimize the presence of the PRERA on the island. Chapter four will provide a detailed analysis of how the programs of the PRERA, such as education, agriculture, and social work, constituted initiatives to establish their scientific and modern knowledge, which in turn transformed the daily lives of the subjects according to the parameters imposed by the colonial state. This chapter explains how the development projects of the PRERA effectively contributed to the establishment of a consensus between New Dealers, local elite, and subaltern sectors of Puerto Rican society that helped to preserve the U.S. colonial regime on the island. Chapter five will provide an explanation of why the developmental programs sponsored by the PRERA "governmentalized" the American colonial rule on the island in the early 1930s. Such process transformed the role of the government and the way in which it exercises power throughout the regulation of the biological aspects of the population. The legacy of such transformation changed the nature of the colonial rule established in 1898 and paved the way to a new rational of government that has lasted until the present day.

Notes

1. "La obra constructiva de la PRERA y sus beneficiosos efectos," *La Rehabilitación,* 3 (Sep, 1935): 1-2, Library of Congress, Washington D.C.
2. The AAA was conceived with the purpose of regulating the production of agricultural goods in order to raise its prices. The extension of its activities to Puerto Rico was disastrous. The island's agricultural economy was based in the production of sugar. As a result, all of the productive lands dedicated to the cultivation of subsistence crops virtually disappeared making the island's population dependant on the importation of food. Consequently, when the prices increases came as a result of the policies of the AAA, thousands of Puerto Ricans were unable to pay for food causing famine in some areas of the island especially those in the countryside. See,

Thomas Mathews, *Puerto Rican Politics and the New Deal* (Gainesville: University of Florida Press, 1960), 132-142.
3. James Mc Gregor Burns, *The Lion and the Fox* (San Diego: Harcourt Brace Jovanovich Publishers, 1956); Richard Hofstadter, *The Age of Reform* (New York: Vintage Books, 1955), Arthur M. Schlesinger, *The Coming of the New Deal* (Boston: Houghton Mifflin Company, 1958), 175., William Leuchtenberg, *Franklin D. Roosevelt and the New Deal* (New York: Harper and Row, 1963).
4. Ronald Radosh and Murray N. Rothard, *A New History of Leviathan: Essays on the Rise of the American Corporate State* (New York: Dutton Paperbacks, 1972); Ellis Hawley, "The Discovery and Study of Corporate Liberalism," *Business History Review* 52 (Autumn 1978): 308-320; Barton Bernstein, *Towards a New Past: Dissenting Essays in American History* (New York: Pantheon Books, 1968); Kim Mc Quaid, "Corporate Liberalism in the American Business Community," *Business History Review* 52 (Autumn 1978): 342-368; Robert Collins. "Positive Responses to the New Deal: The Roots of the Committee for Economic Development, 1933-42," *Business History Review* (autumn, 1978): 368-390; Louis Galambos, "Technology, Political Economy, and Professionalization: Central Themes of the Organizational Synthesis," *Business Historical Review* 57 (Winter 1983): 471-491, Barton Bernstein, *Towards a New Past: Dissenting Essays in American History* (New York: Pantheon Books, 1968).
5. Steve Fraser and Gary Gerstle, *The Rise and Fall of the New Deal Order* (Princeton: Princeton University Press, 1989); Lizabeth Cohen, *Making a New Deal: Industrial Workers in Chicago, 1919-1939* (New York Cambridge University Press, 1990); Suzanne Mettler, *Dividing Citizens: Gender and Federalism in New Deal Public Policy* (Ithaca: Cornell University Press, 1998); Alan Brinkley, *The End of the Reform: New Deal Liberalism in Recession and War* (New York: Alfred A. Knopf, 1995); Rebecca Skalaroff Laureen, *Black Culture and the New Deal: The Quest of for Civil Rights in the Roosevelt Era* Chapel Hill: The University of North Carolina Press, 2009; Roger Biles, *The South and the New Deal* Lexington: University of Kentucky Press, 2006; Neil Maher, *Nature's New Deal: The Civilian Conservation Corps and the Roots of the American Environmental Movement* New York: Oxford University Press, 2008; William Chafe, The Achievement of American Liberalism The New Deal and its Legacies New York: Columbia University Press, 2003.
6. Thomas Mathews, *Puerto Rican Politics and the New Deal* (Gainesville: University of Florida Press, 1960).
7. Gordon Lewis, *Freedom and Power in the Caribbean* (New York: Monthly Review Press, 1963).
8. Ibid., 129.
9. Ibid., 141.

10. See, Arturo Morales Carrión, *Puerto Rico a Political and Cultural History* (New York: W.W. Norton, 1983), 220-225.
11. Fernando Picó, *Historia general de Puerto Rico* (Río Piedras: Editorial Huracán, 1986), 246, James Dietz, *Economic History of Puerto Rico: Institutional Change and Capitalist Development* (Princeton: Princeton University Press, 1986), 154-158, Blanca Silvestrini and Dolores Luque, *Historia de Puerto Rico: trayectoria de un pueblo* (San Juan: Ediciones Cultural Panamericana, 1988), 483-489, Francisco Scarano, *Puerto Rico: cinco siglos de historia* (San Juan: McGraw Hill, 1993), 676-683.
12. Blanca Silvestrini, *Los trabajadores puertorriqueños y el Partido Socialista* (Río Piedras: Editorial Universidad, 1979), 11; César Rey, "Parlamentarismo Obrero y Coalición 1932-1940," in *Senado de Puerto Rico: ensayos de historia constitucional 1917-1992*, ed. Carmen Raffuci, Silvia Álvarez Curbelo, and Fernando Picó (Río Piedras: Ediciones Huracán, 1992), 140. *Taller de Formación Política, Huelga en la caña 1933-34* (Río Piedras: Ediciones Huracán, 1982), 12; Taller de Formación Política, *No estamos pidiendo el cielo, huelga portuaria de 1938* (Río Piedras: Ediciones Huracán, 1988), 194-197.
13. A substantial portion of the traditional New Deal studies in Puerto Rico has been devoted to the political struggles of the Liberal and Coalition Parties for the control of the PRERA and PRRA on the island. This book will present these controversies in a historiographical context in order to provide the reader with the general conditions of politics on the island (chapters 2 and 3). It is not the intent of this book to devote extensive attention to the interaction between the New Deal and local politics, a topic already studied and thoroughly exhausted.
14. James Ferguson, *The Antipolitics Machine, Development, Depoliticization, and Bureaucratic Power in Lesotho* (Minneapolis: University of Minnesota Press, 1994).
15. Stacey Pigg, "Constructing Social Categories through Place: Social Representation and Development in Nepal," *Comparative Studies in Society and History* 34 (1992): 491-513.
16. Arturo Escobar, *Encountering Development: The Making and Unmaking of the Third World* Princeton: Princeton University Press), 10.
17. Escobar, 9.
18. Ibid., 10.
19. Escobar, 45. As Arturo Escobar pointed out, "The concept of professionalization refers mainly to the process that brings the Third World into the politics of expert knowledge and Western science in general. This is accomplished through a set of techniques, strategies, and disciplinary practices that organize the generation, validation, and diffusion of development knowledge, including the academic disciplines, methods of research and teaching, criteria of expertise, and manifold professional practices; in other

words, those mechanisms through the which a politics of truth is created and maintained."
20. Graham Burchell, Colin Gordon and Peter Miller, *Foucault Effect Studies in Governmentality* (Chicago: University of Chicago Press, 1991), 103.
21. Burchell, *The Foucault Effect,* 102-103.
22. Burchell, *The Foucault Effect,* 100.
23. Burchell, *The Foucault Effect*, 100.
24. Michel Foucault, *Defender la sociedad* (México D.F. Fondo de Cultura Económica, 2002), 217-237.
25. Michel Foucault, *Historia de la sexualidad la voluntad de saber* (México D. F.: Siglo XXI, Vol. 1, 1977), 168-169.
26. Foucault, *Historia de la sexualidad*, 169.
27. Until 1934 Puerto Rico was under the jurisdiction of the War Department. That year it was transferred to the Department of Interior, Bureau of Office and Territories in charge of the administration of the US territories.
28. Perhaps the most lamentable case is the one of James Bourne, Administrator of the PRERA. The only publication in which Bourne has a small participation is in a study of the 1960s written with his wife where they analyze the influence of the social service department of the PRERA and the PRRA on similar programs sponsored by the Popular Democratic Party during from the 1940s to the 1960. Little mention is made about his overall experience as administrator of the PRERA. Dorothy Bourne, *Thirty Years of Change in Puerto Rico; a Case Study of Ten Selected Rural Areas by Dorothy Dulles Bourne and James R. Bourne* (New York: F.A. Praeger, 1966).

CHAPTER 1

Bringing the Promise of Modernity: A New Deal for Puerto Rico, 1932-1935

The Arrival of the Depression in Puerto Rico, 1929-1933

Improvements in the fields of education, health, and infrastructure, experienced in the first two decades of the twentieth century, certainly were not enough to substantially improve the material and political conditions of thousands of Puerto Ricans. Puerto Rico experienced the conversion of its agricultural wealth into a one-crop sugar economy and the rapid proletarianization of its working force. Such transformations had a detrimental impact on Puerto Ricans, condemning thousands of them to the most abject poverty.[1] The Treaty of Paris and the later approval of the Foraker and Jones Acts completed this economic and political setting, providing the legal grounds for the establishment of a colonial regime that legitimized the capitalist logic established on the island in the early years of the previous century. More than the enlightened civilization promised by General Miles in 1898, the United States would be better described as historian Gordon Lewis argues as an "imperialism of neglect."

By the early 1930s the Depression in Puerto Rico led to a rapid deterioration of the local economy and rising social tensions that threatened the stability of the colonial relationship. Three decades of U.S. domination had changed the economic landscape of Puerto Rico. Sugar constituted the main source of economic revenue, followed by coffee, tobacco, and small fruit production.[2] Another area that registered a major development in terms of production was the garment industry. Since the beginning of the century, a growing demand on the East coast of the United States stimulated the development of the Puerto Rican garment industry, considered by many to be of excellent quality. A substantial portion of the population, mainly women and children, were employed in this industry during the 1930s, making of it one of the most profitable business of the local economy.[3] Public works also constituted an important but often overlooked sector of Puerto Rico's economy during the 1920s and early 1930s. By 1929 an estimated $50,000,000 were invested in public works around the island, providing thousands of jobs. For officials, the jobs provided by the public sphere provided social "thrift" to a large population without steady work. Therefore, they warned about an eventual saturation in this sector that would certainly impact the already deteriorated economy of Puerto Rico.[4]

These changes in the local economy had a profound and tragic impact on the living conditions in Puerto Rico at the beginning of the 1930s. In urban areas, the landscape was dotted with slums and poverty-stricken living conditions. Skilled workers usually had the best living conditions within the urban areas, with earnings of $1 to $3 dollars per day. They lived in relatively comfortable four-room houses in suburban areas. The story was different for unskilled laborers who lived in the unsanitary conditions of huts made of disposed materials. They earned wages of less than one dollar per day. The higher wages in the urban centers did not improve the conditions of poverty for many of the members of the unskilled labor class, even though their salaries were often higher than in those of the countryside.[5] The rural areas of the island reflected the terrible impact of a proletarianization process that commenced in the 1910s with the emergence of the sugar industry. Many peasants, or *jíbaros,* on the island lacked any sort of land title or property and, as a result they lived as *agregados* in the property of an owner.[6] The housing conditions of this rural population were poor and miserable as well, as described by Dr. Victor Clark:

"The commonest type of Puerto Rican laborer's house today is a framework of pole and scantling, nailed or tied with native fiber. The walls may be of boards, thatch, or the bark or galvanized iron. The floors are made of boards and generally raised a few feet from the ground. Such a hut must frequently stand on the side of a hill, and the raised flooring permits the water from the torrential rains to pass down the hillside, carrying what litter may have accumulated. It has no ceiling. It has no kitchen, except a lean-to on the outside, without flooring and partly open to the weather and containing a few stones thrown together for a stove."[7]

Other rural workers, especially in the sugar industry, lived in barracks during the sugar cane harvest, or *zafra*.[8] The wages earned by these workers merely maintained their families. Most of the rural workers were employed on a seasonal basis. The sugar cane *zafra* lasted from the months of January to July, tobacco from December to January, and coffee from August to September. By December 1929, 36 percent of the population was unemployed. The average sugar worker wages were from $.60 $1.25 per day. In the tobacco industry both women and men had wages of just $1.00 a day. In the fruit industry, where the majority of the workers were women and children, the wages fluctuated between 50 cent to $1.00 for nine hours of labor. For children the wages fluctuated from 20 to 26 cent a day during the cultivation process, with a small increase in packing-related jobs. Such wages did not keep up with the high prices of imported foodstuffs for the basic necessities of the average Puerto Rican family. According to studies conducted in 1930, the Puerto Rican peasant devoted 94 % of his income to food and left the remaining 4 % for other essentials of life.[9] If we take into consideration that the typical Puerto Rican rural family of that time averaged 8.1 persons per family, it can be concluded that such wages did not satisfy the basic necessities. The deterioration of health conditions among the island inhabitants also presented a grim picture. Despite the decline in mortality death rates, some diseases such as diarrhea, tuberculosis, and malaria still took a huge toll among the peasant population, especially among children.[10]

Education in Puerto Rico was another area that faced serious problems during the early 1930s. By that time, the educational system that prevailed on the island could not keep up with the demand of new students. Despite a population of approximately 500,000 students, the Puerto Rican system had the facilities to accommodate only 220,000.[11] By the end of the 1920s, the conditions of the Puerto Rican peasantry were summarized in a succinct but appealing fashion:

> "There is a degree of submissiveness to misfortune and a lack of class feeling that to an outside observer is difficult to understand. Perhaps it is the widespread illness, perhaps it is the background of slavery and feudalism, perhaps it is the extreme poverty, perhaps the terrific impact of the periodic storms that carry all away with them and make human effort and ingenuity seem like naught, which explains the passive helplessness of the rural community."[12]

On the other side of the social spectrum, upper and middle class sectors were also affected by the dramatic transformations in the economic conditions of the island that eroded their material base of power.[13] The early 1930s witnessed the growth of a Puerto Rican professional sector and a corporate bureaucracy that supported the operations of the sugar industry as had been happening since the early 1900s. The integration of the Puerto Rican economy to the U.S. market, particularly in the agricultural area, sponsored the emergence of an entrepreneurial and commercial sector that served as intermediaries in commercial transactions between the two countries.[14]

By the early 1930s, the *colonos* cultivated about 48.7 percent of the land devoted to the cultivation of sugar and produced about 35.5% of the sugar refined in Puerto Rico.[15] During the 1930s, this sector experienced serious economic problems as a result of the competence of U.S. capital outside (absentee capital) Puerto Rico and the instability of the sugar international markets. The *colonos* represented the last elements of the displaced sugar *hacendado* class of the nineteenth century. In the long run, the members of this class sold their rural properties and immigrated to the urban centers to facilitate the education of their sons and daughters. As a result, the former *hacendado* class started to penetrate the occupational niche of the professional ranks.[16] By the early 1940s, the second generation of this displaced *hacendado* class had chance to recover its hegemonic base with the emergence of the colonial populist state and the growing demand of a technocrat sector willing to establish its programs.

The Political Landscape

The major social and economic changes experienced by Puerto Rico under U.S. colonialism inevitably brought significant alterations to the island's political life. Politics moved from conditions of shifting alliances to ones of violence and transformations under the enormous impact of the Great Depression. Such changes were manifested in three important ways: 1. the odd alliance between the Republican and Socialist Parties; 2. the cooperation of some members of the Liberal Party with the Roosevelt administration to articulate a reconstruction plan for the island; 3. the politics of violence and confrontation of the Nationalist Party.

First, the emergence of new and fragile alliances between corporate and working class sectors of Puerto Rican society changed the local political landscape. The remnants of the former Union Party and the Republican Party formed the *Unión Republicana* (Republican Union Party) in January of 1932.[17] In the midst of all these political changes another political emerged in October, 1932. The Republican Union and the Socialist Party, fearing a victory of the *liberales* (liberals), joined forces in the *Coalición* (Coalition) to participate in the elections of November, 1932. The reason for such an odd alliance between these traditional enemies was based on the "deplorable economic, social, political, and industrial conditions experienced by the island in this moment" and to break the influence that the Union Party had.[18] Despite the differences between the Republican Union and the Socialist Party in terms of class composition, both parties agreed to preserve their own political platform and party integrity.[19] The chain of events that followed the formation of this peculiar political alliance proved to be successful. By November of 1932, the Coalition won the insular elections, maintaining power for the rest of the decade.[20] Despite the provisions of both parties to preserve its ideological integrity and platforms, the class interests of each of the coalition partner's class interests between

Socialists and Republicans posed contradictory positions. The Republican ranks were made of up of professionals and members of the local corporate elite.[21] In contrast, the Socialists were blue collar workers who taught that access and participation in insular political power was worth the risks of an alliance with their traditional antagonist class.[22] When the time came and the labor legislation sponsored by the New Deal (NRA, the Wagner Act, and the FLSA) were extended to the island, a strong opposition from the Republican ranks of the Coalition tried to impede its implementation, pushing the Socialist leadership into a difficult predicament with respect to the demands of its members.[23] As historian Blanca Silvestrini pointed out, a breach between the working class bureaucracy and its power base was opened. Such a breach in the long run would demonstrate the fragility of the Coalition and its eventual dissolution in 1940.[24]

A second important transformation in the local political arena was the cooperation of some members of the Liberal Party with the Roosevelt administration in the articulation of a plan to transform Puerto Rico's socio-economic conditions. Luis Muñoz Marín, by then elected senator for the Liberal Party, was a key element for this new understanding between members of the local political elite and the Roosevelt administration. The son of Luis Muñoz Rivera, founder of the Union Party and a former Resident Commissioner in Washington, D.C. Muñoz Marín was exposed at an early age to the intricate Washington political atmosphere.[25] For Muñoz, a militant of the Socialist Party during the 1920s, the New Deal represented an opportunity to bring social and economic reform to Puerto Rico:

> "The potentialities of the New Deal to face the vital problems of Puerto Rico appear to me more evident. I am not talking about of applying all its policies, but I think that there are numerous elements that can be applied in a constructive way to the exigencies of reform of the island."[26]

During the 1930s, Muñoz communicated constantly with New Dealers and influenced the implementation of many of its programs. Indeed, the Coalition resented that a member of a minority party ran many of the New Deal policies on the island and saw him as a challenge to its power. The Coalition maintained that the Liberals used the New Deal resources (especially the PRERA) to establish a parallel government that challenged the institutional initiatives of its administration. The intervention of Muñoz symbolized the beginning of a new era of cooperation between sectors of the Puerto Rican political elite and the United States. Eventually the fruits of such cooperation would culminate in the decisive support of the Roosevelt administration for the PRRA development initiatives and the populist reform programs implemented by Muñoz Marín in the early 1940s.

A third change in local politics was practiced by the Nationalist Party and its politics of violence and confrontation. Other political tendencies assumed a seminal role in Puerto Rico's political scenery. During the 1920s, the Union Party was the only political organization that included in its ideological platform the status of independence for Puerto Rico. By 1922, the party changed its political interest and decided to support an ideological platform based on a "free associated state" or commonwealth. As a result of such a change in its political platform, many members of the Union Party who had supported independence founded the Nationalist Party in April, 1922.[27] This secession within the ranks of the Union Party worsened when in 1924 this political organization formed a political alliance with the Republican Party. This event caused the definite separation of the Nationalists from the Union Party and allowed a young lawyer just graduated from Harvard, Pedro Albizu Campos, to assume the leadership of this new political organization. In a party congress in May of 1930, a more militant posture against U.S. domination of the island was proposed by Albizu Campos. Albizu's political project advocated the overthrow of the U.S. colonial regime, the elimination of the teaching of English in the classroom, and opposition to any attempt to make Puerto Rico a state. Albizu proposed that the political platform of the Nationalist Party include a reorganization of the party. He wanted the organization of workers to demand better working conditions, and he denounced the negative impact of the U.S. absentee capital on the island's economy.[28] As a result of the defeat of the Nationalist Party in 1932, Albizu and its organization decided to assume a more militant posture against the presence of the United States on the island. Acts of violence between Nationalist Party members and federal authorities on the island were registered throughout the 1930s.[29] In 1937, Albizu was accused by federal authorities of participating in the murder of the Colonel of the Insular Police Elisha Riggs, as well as of a conspiracy, recruitment of military personnel to overthrow the U.S. authority on the island, and inciting rebellion against federal authorities.[30] As a result, Albizu and other prominent members of the Nationalist Party were condemned to ten years of prison in a Federal penitentiary in Atlanta.[31] Many debates have raged as a result of the activities of the Nationalist Party in Puerto Rico during the 1930. The Nationalist Party perhaps is the best evidence of the fragility of the colonial relationship between the United States and Puerto Rico. Despite the difficult economic conditions brought by the Depression and the acceptance of its discourse by substantial sectors of the population, the nationalists were unable to capitalize on the collapse of the conditions of the island as a byproduct of the colonial situation between the United States and the island.[32]

The Quest for a Colonial Relationship

The crisis of the early 1930s exposed the fragility of the colonial regime established by the Americans in Puerto Rico since 1898. By the early 1930s, the U.S. government soon understood that a new model of colonialism had to be implemented in order to preserve its possession in the Caribbean. Some sectors of the U.S. bureaucracy dealing with Puerto Rican affairs suggested diverse colonial models in an attempt to preserve the United States presence in Puerto Rico. The first model that I want to discuss is the one proposed by Rexford Tugwell. For Tugwell, one of the most important problems was the lack of a "colonial policy" toward the island and the bureaucratic inefficiency to deal with its problems.[33] In a period of three decades, the island was under the jurisdiction of the State Department, the War Department and, finally, under the division of Territories and Possessions of the Department of the Interior. For many Puerto Ricans, especially the political elite, such institutional ambiguity caused confusion and lack of coordination with respect to the federal policies applied to the island. In addition, local economic sectors felt underrepresented and betrayed by this bureaucratic web.[34] The commentaries of Tugwell suggest that by 1933, federal authorities were concerned that the relations between

Puerto Rico and the United States had to be modified in order to keep the island politically stable during the difficult times of the Depression. The transfer of Puerto Rico from the War Department to the Department of the Interior in 1934 constituted the first bureaucratic action to extend a coordinated federal initiative in order to improve the socioeconomic conditions of the island under the direction of a civil branch of the federal government. Yet, more than an administrative transfer had to be done in order to fix three decades of neglectful colonialism.

The second initiative to improve the colonial conditions of the island by the beginning of the 1930s was the one offered by Dr. Victor Clark, the man in charge of the study sponsored by the Brookings Institution for the study of the economic and social conditions in Puerto Rico. Clark's recommendations echoed Tugwell's and were directed to the reorganization of the bureaucratic presence of the federal government on the island in the areas of insular government, health, and education. Without reference to the colonial situation between the island and the United States, Clark made clear in his study that changes in the relationship between the United States and Puerto Rico were necessary because of the cultural differences between the two countries:

> "Two dissimilar cultures are in the process of mutual assimilation within the island. Its people constitute a relatively small and isolated community vividly conscious of its individuality, and they are correspondingly jealous of its special character and privileges. They may be politically divided among themselves but they are instinctively stood together against the outside world. Naturally, therefore, they wish to direct their own affairs. Their desire to do so is not anti-American but American. In a broad sense, the present study points the way toward a complete realization of this ambition, by building up an educated and economically independent citizenry and by governmental reforms that will make the legislative and administrative machinery more manageable and efficient."[35]

For Clark, the problem of Puerto Rico resided not in its cultural differences but in the lack of interest of the U.S. government in assuming its institutional responsibility over the island. According to Clark, Puerto Ricans were pro-American individuals that were willing to assume the direction of their own destiny. The solution proposed by this scholar pointed out to the imperative necessity of implementing an efficient governmental bureaucracy that led the economic and social development of the island. Certainly the establishment of the PRERA as a development initiative constituted a partial solution to such a problem.

A third initiative, proposed by former Governor of the island, Theodore Roosevelt, Jr., was concerned with the future nature of the colonial relationship between the United States and Puerto Rico in 1929. Discarding statehood and independence as real alternatives to Puerto Rico's political status, Roosevelt suggested a "dominion status" as a solution to the colonial dilemma. According to Roosevelt, in order to have established this dominion status in Puerto Rico, it would have been necessary to accept the fact that the island was a different cultural entity. In order to establish this domination status, or enlighten colonialism, it was necessary first to discontinue any attempt to remodel Puerto Ricans "so that they should become similar in language habits and thoughts to continental Americans" and a reformulation of the fiscal policies imposed on the island in order to provide enough sources for the necessities of the local government.[36] In addition to these suggestions, Roosevelt also envisioned that the relationship between the United States and Puerto Rico was considered as a diplomatic asset, a link between the United States and other Latin American countries. As Roosevelt suggested, Puerto Ricans might have been a "connecting link," a "show window looking to the south", in which Puerto Ricans "acquainted with America and America's method of thought will be ideally suited for representatives of American banking or industries in the Latin American countries."[37] This "dominion" status, according to Roosevelt, constituted "farsighted colonial policies of the future may possibly contain a still further objective, namely the organization of dissimilar people on a dominion status. This may be the ultimate answer to many of the vexatious problems that confront the world today."[38] The proposal of Roosevelt suggested another perspective about the colonial relation between the United States and Puerto Rico. The former governor envisioned Puerto Rico as a bridge that would be used by the United States to articulate a new approach towards the relations with Latin America, preserving intact the colonial status of the island.

By the early 1930s, the Puerto Rican colonial dilemma remained unsolved. A growing sector of Puerto Ricans began to question the legitimacy of such political status, creating an environment of social tension and disappointment. However by 1933, the PRERA emerged as new strategy of colonial domination. The emergence of this agency was an answer to the concern of U.S. officials to establish a rational colonial regime, able to deal with the complex problems of the island. The imperialism of neglect was substituted by a well-articulated development program that after almost three decades of American institutional presence in Puerto Rico, they reshaped the image of the federal government in the critical times brought by the Great Depression.

The New Deal in Puerto Rico

At the same time that the organizational and funding bases of the PRERA were extended to Puerto Rico, other New Deal agencies reached the island's shores at the beginning of the 1930s. However, the existence of these agencies has been constantly overlooked by previous historical narratives. In order to provide a general overview of how other New Deal agencies on the island coexisted with the PRERA, I will devote the following pages to a succinct examination of the most important controversies that involved the Agricultural Adjustment Act (AAA) and the National Recovery Administration (NRA). These bureaucratic units faced numerous logistical problems and legal controversies that caused their disappearance from the institutional scene or minimized their ability to solve the problems for which they were created.[39] In many cases, the controversies that these agencies experienced in the continental United States were inevitably inherited by their counterparts in Puerto Rico. In the particular case of Puerto Rico, these conditions were aggravated because the spirit of the legislation often overlooked the precarious and special conditions that the island presented as a territorial possession. As a result, the initial New Deal presence in Puerto Rico presented an unorganized and chaotic view that to some extent made this topic be avoided by traditional historical narratives.

The implementation of the AAA, which was approved by Congress in May, 1933, exemplifies this hectic scenario. The effects of this legislation began to be felt in Puerto Rico in the summer of 1933. Designed to raise the prices of agricultural products to the standards prevailing from 1909 to 1929, Title I of the legislation imposed a "processing tax" on agricultural surpluses and subsidized farmers for the destruction of crops and the maintenance of uncultivated tracks of land in an effort to avoid overproduction.[40] Such legislation affected Puerto Rico in two ways. First, consumers on the island had to pay elevated prices since Puerto Rico imported a considerable amount of basic agricultural products from the United States, especially wheat, flour, rice, codfish, and meat, most of these products were subject to taxation as a result of the AAA legislation.[41] This process considerably impacted a population already heavily struck by the Depression and with an already low income.[42] Second, Puerto Rican farmers were not covered by the benefits of the law because most of the products were not produced on the island, but were imported, thus depriving them of the opportunity to be compensated by federal funds.[43] The Governor of the island at that time, Robert Gore, was among the people who complained about the implementation of the statutes of the AAA on the island. "According to Gore, the AAA legislation represented a "tremendous hardship to Puerto Rico" in terms of its harmful effects to the island's economy."[44] Attorney General Norman Thomings, promptly responded to Governor Gore's concern by saying "that any tax imposed under the AAA, would apply to the domestic processing of a commodity for export to Puerto Rico and also that there is no method by which Puerto Rico could be relieved of the possible effects of such tax, except by action of the Congress."[45] Despite the strong opposition of the business sectors and the U.S. governor, the statutes of the AAA continued to be enforced in Puerto Rico.

Diverse sectors in Puerto Rican society feared that the implementation of the AAA would worsen the already devastated economy. These sectors pleaded to the local U.S. authorities and the United States Congress to exempt Puerto Rico from the legislation. The Chamber of Commerce and the Association of Industrialists were among these sectors. His president, Filipo de Hostos, warned Governor Blanton Winship about the dangerous situation created on the island as a result of the implementation of the AAA.[46] Hostos proposed an amendment to the AAA, which would eliminate the processing tax imposed on local manufacturers for basic foodstuffs. In addition, Hostos warned the U.S. authorities about the harmful effects in the garment, fruit, and cotton industries.[47] The Association of Industrialists and its president, Lupercio Colberg, joined Hostos in his arguments of the potential problems posed by the AAA. As Colberg pointed out, the AAA caused a considerable reduction of the mercantile transactions and the production capacity of the country, the suppression of bank credit, and a reduction in general spending and personnel. Colberg demanded swift action in order to avoid a catastrophe that the government could not control, condemning 1,500,000 citizens to misery.[48] The AAA also attacked one of the pillars of the Puerto Rican economy during the 1930s: the sugar production industry.

Because sugar did not qualify as a basic necessity under the AAA standards, its production was subject to regulation.[49] In order to enforce the limitation of production, the President, in accordance with the AAA, proposed in January of 1934, the Costigan-Jones Act, and a law aimed at the regulation of sugar production. According to the Costigan-Jones Act, the price of sugar would be stabilized, and a fair share of sugar production would be distributed in the form of quotas to the producers in the U.S. territories and possessions: Louisiana (beet sugar producers), the Philippines, Hawaii, Cuba, and Puerto Rico.[50] As a result, the Puerto Rican quota was reduced from 875,000 to 821,000 tons.[51]

Businessmen and U.S. officials were not the only ones concerned about the implementation of the Act. The Costigan Act was a subject of concern throughout the ranks of the labor organizations. For Prudencio Rivera Martínez, labor commissioner of Puerto Rico, and to Rafael Alonso Torres, Chairman of the Finance committee of the House of Representative of Puerto Rico, the Costigan Act posed a threat to the stability of the Puerto Rican labor force.[52] According to these officials, the application of the Costigan Act would cause the dismissal of about 16,000 workers in the sugar industry.[53] In order to avoid this situation, Rivera and Alonso proposed a series of provisions, such as reassigning federal funds from other New Deal programs to pay wages to displaced workers, enforcing the statutes of the law forbidding child labor, and providing incentives for farms to diversify agriculture. They also suggested that the minimum wage for the following year (1935) be determined by the administration in an effort to avoid industrial "unrest".[54]

The impact of the Costigan Act was felt among all the sectors of Puerto Rican society involved in the sugar industry. In order to fight the implementation of this law, U.S. officials and Puerto Ricans alike utilized the extension of the U.S. citizenship to Puerto Rico in 1917 as a strategy to defend the existing sugar quota production. These sectors thought that invoking the U.S. citizenship imposed upon them they would get a better chance to increase their production quota with respect to other foreign competitors. This strategy is demonstrated by people such as Jorge Bird Arias, administrative employee of the Fajardo Sugar Company of Puerto Rico, when he complained about the unfairness of the production quota assigned to Puerto Rico in relation to other U.S. possessions. According to Bird, Puerto Rico had been treated as the "Cinderella of the family."[55] The Farmers Association of Puerto Rico complained about the imposition of the Costigan Act and its harmful effects on the island's sugar economy. As a basis of their argument, the Farmers Association accused the United States of considering Puerto Rico as a foreign country: "Puerto Rico is primarily opposed to this legislation because it is classed with and treated in the same manner as a foreign country. The island feels that this bill does not accord it to the rights to which it is without question entitled as a community of American citizens."[56] Puerto Rican sugar sectors did not hesitate in utilizes the U.S. citizenship in order to defend their interests. Thus, U.S. citizenship became a valuable strategy against the discrimination of the metropolitan state regarding the authorization of the sugar quotas. Even federal authorities in Puerto Rico complained about the implementation of the sugar regulation legislation, including Governor Blanton Winship. The governor argued that the implementation of such quotas would be affected by the arrival of a hurricane with the potential to disrupt the sugar quota.[57] Winship pointed out that, in the case of a hurricane:

> "The Bill and the maximum quota that could be conceded to Puerto Rico would be unreasonably short due to hurricane years having been included in estimate average production. This would aggravate unemployment."[58]

Besides the potential threat posed by natural disaster as a deterrent for the imposition of the sugar quota, Winship did not hesitate to use the U.S. citizenship as a strategy to avoid the implementation of the Costigan law on the island. Like the Puerto Rican Farmers Association before, Winship pointed out that Puerto Ricans were U.S. citizens that worked their own cane fields, in contrast with that practice of Cuban producers who imported Jamaican and Haitian workers to their sugar fields.[59]

Some sectors had another perspective about the U.S citizenship and its use to defend the sugar industry. According to Aboy Martínez, president of the Association of Sugar Producers, the rise in prices proposed by the AAA was equivalent to a continuous rise in the prices of raw materials and foodstuffs as well as the reduction of labor hours and the salary raise proposed by the administration. As a result, if the island was excluded from the policies of the AAA, it could gain temporary relief from the effects of inflation. In the long term however, it would increase the harmful effects of a rise in the cost of living.[60] Martínez firmly believed that Puerto Rico had a responsibility to participate in the AAA legislation because of its "political" relationship with the United States. According to Martínez, Puerto Rico, as part of the United States, had the duty to respond positively to the initiatives of President Roosevelt in order to face the harmful effects of the Depression:

> "We do not believe that it is convenient for Puerto Rico not to cooperate with a national emergency program. We Puerto Ricans have a citizenship that compels us to struggle shoulder to shoulder with our fellow countrymen of the continent, especially in these times when it is necessary to reestablish the national normality."[61]

Martínez offered another perspective regarding the utilization of U.S. citizenship as a strategy to support and validate the sugar industry interests. For him, the U.S. citizenship meant not a strategy to get a waiver from the sugar quotas, but an opportunity to "struggle shoulder-to-shoulder with our fellow countrymen" an opportunity to demonstrate to the United States the commitment of Puerto Ricans to the Roosevelt administration in its effort to overcome the terrible economic effects of the Depression. It is important to note how the implementation of the AAA made U.S. citizenship an important issue to be used against the threat of this legislation in local sugar interests. The controversies generated as a result of the implementation of the AAA in Puerto Rico allow us to appreciate how Puerto Ricans had multiple perspectives about the possible uses of their citizenship and how it can be used on their behalf, regardless of their colonial condition.

Similar to the AAA, the NRA reflected the same problems, confusions, and contradictions inherent to the experimental nature of the New Deal policies in Puerto Rico. Such confusions and contradictions were enhanced by the difficult situation of the Puerto Rican economy, the apathy of businessmen, low wages, and the peculiar situation of local politics. Many of the industries that epitomized the fragile island's economy, such as the garment and sugar industries, depended on low wages and onerous conditions of work to generate enough profit to compete in international markets and to guarantee their own existence.[62] To add more confusion to the situation, the arrival of the NRA coincided with one of the most intensive strike periods ever experienced in Puerto Rico's history.[63] Notwithstanding, the NRA was implemented in the summer of 1933. Again, the Association of Industrialists assumed leadership in the articulation of a corporate front against the NRA. On July 10, 1933, the Association wrote to General Hugh Johnson, head of the NRA, telling him about the disastrous effects of the application of the NRA in Puerto Rico. According to Lupercio Colberg, president of the Association, Puerto Rican industries had the right to organize their own industries because the economic condition of the island was different from that of the continental United States. The application of industrial codes by the United States, according to Colberg, would represent "the material destruction of our industries and will stop the progress of Puerto Rico as an industrial community."[64] For Colberg, the imposition of the codes and by the United States was an act of injustice that "will be satisfactory for the Americans but not to Puerto Rico considering the present conditions."[65]

Perhaps the most significant impact of the NRA on the island was noticed in the local political arena. As we discussed, the Socialist Party and the Free Federation of Labor that represented the island workers were allied with the Republican Party, an organization that represented the industrial and economic interests of a good portion of the dominant circles of Puerto Rican society. The NRA accentuated the antagonism among these political allies. On the one hand, the Free Federation of Labor was sympathetic to the labor legislation proposed by the Roosevelt administration. On the other hand, as it happened in the United States, the first sector that protested against this legislation was that of the business elite and corporate interests, prominent members of the Republican faction within the governing coalition. Meanwhile, the Free Federation of Labor supported the NRA unconditionally; especially section 7(a) that granted workers the right to unionize. On July 20, 1933, the Free Federation clearly manifested its position toward the law:

> "It is our purpose to look that this law be complied with. I suggest that if the Puerto Rican industrials do not confer with their workers in the section of the code that deals with wages and minimum hours, they (the workers) should contact General Hugh Johnson administrator of the NRA with the purpose of be heard by him in the discussion of the codes in dispute."[66]

The presence of the NRA would have its effect the fragile coalition of the Republican and Socialist Party as happened with the implementation of the Fair Labor Standards Act.[67]

The New Deal in Puerto Rico represented, at least in its initial period, a confusing, contradictory, and fragmentary mosaic that, instead of presenting hope, presented a continuity of the chaotic conditions brought upon by the Depression and a rapid deterioration of the colonial relationship with the United States. The confusion and impracticability of the initial New Deal legislation proved unsuccessful in solving the economic chaos of the Depression or improving significantly the living conditions of Puerto Ricans. This situation worsened in 1935 when the U.S. Supreme Court declared both the AAA and the NRA unconstitutional. To some extent, the uncoordinated New Deal initiatives, represented through the AAA and the NRA, strengthened the position of the PRERA as the only coherent and coordinated New Deal agency on the island at the time. As a result, this agency absorbed and integrated other New Deal programs, especially the ones devoted to the distribution and coordination of public works and social assistance t the unemployed population of the island.[68] One of the elements that contributed to the PRERA's structural cohesiveness was its careful planning and its capacity to encompass the functions of other New Deal agencies under one coordinated structure. This organizational rationale was in great part responsible for how the PRERA reached all sectors of the island and had a considerable impact on Puerto Rican society.

Notes

1. Rexford Tugwell, *The Stricken Land* (New York: Doubleday and Company, 1947), 72-75. In his book, *The Stricken Land* Rexford Tugwell provides a description of the poverty conditions of the Puerto Rico.
2. Bailey Diffie and Justine Diffie. *Porto Rico: A Broken Pledge* (New York: The Vanguard Press, 1931), 45-106. For the year 1930, the sugar crop reached about 865, 109 tons. Four major absentee companies owned virtually the totality of this production: The South Porto Rico Sugar Company, The Fajardo Sugar Company, the *Central Aguirre* Sugar Company, and the United Porto Rican Sugar Company. These companies possessed about one fifth of the total wealth of the island and 67 percent of the agricultural wealth. Tobacco and small fruit production also constituted important sectors of the Puerto Rican economy. By 1929, this crop reached a cultivation of 30, 000 acres. Similar to the sugar situation, the tobacco business was in the hands by absentee American companies. About 80 to 85% of the tobacco business was manufactured by these companies: The Porto Rican American Tobacco Company of New Jersey, The Porto Rican American Tobacco Company of Puerto Rico, The Congress Cigar Company and the New York-Tampa Cigar Company. Small fruit industry registered a rapid growth by the early 1930s. By that time about 10, 000 acres were produced, especially grapefruit and oranges. As a difference from the sugar and tobacco sector, the fruit industry company presented a more balance picture in terms of capital ownership. Of the 46 companies, 28 were owned by Americans and 18 by Puerto Ricans.
3. James Dietz, *Economic History of Puerto Rico: Institutional Change and Capitalist Development* (Princeton: Princeton University Press, 1986), 142-143. By 1930, the per capita income for a rural Puerto Rican family was $270.00-$275.00 per year. An average woman wage in the needlework industry averaged 8.9 cents an hour and $ 3.32 a week. Home needle workers had even lower wages averaging 2 cents an hour or less during the same period.
4. Victor S. Clark, *Porto Rico and its Problems* (Washington, D.C.: The Brookings Institution, 1930), xxi.

5. Clark, 39-50.
6. Clark, 14. The term *agregado* generally means a land-less peasant.
7. Clark, 15-16.
8. The *zafra,* or harvesting of the sugar cane was conducted from the months of June to September.
9. Diffie and Diffie, 162-183.
10. Report of Governor Theodore Roosevelt, Jr. *Thirtieth Annual Report of the Governor of Puerto Rico,* Aug 21, 1930, U.S. Government Printing Office, University of New York, Hunter College, New York. By Jun 30, 1929 the administration of Governor Roosevelt Jr. reported about 4,442 deaths from tuberculosis as well as 200,000 cases of malaria and 600,000 of hookworm.
11. Theodore Roosevelt, Jr. *Thirtieth Annual Report of the Governor of Puerto Rico,* 5-6. For a comparative perspective of the conditions of the Puerto Rican educational system in the late 1890s, see Diffie and Diffie, 25-26. The Puerto Rican education system also had to face other serious problems during the first three decades of U.S. domination. Education was more accessible to the urban population as a result of the strong investment made by the government, but in the rural areas the case was the opposite. Many of the children in the countryside were sick, poorly clothed and ill-nourished. Also, the employers often posed obstacles to the education of the peasantry, arguing that such advancement could impact the source of labor. Some members of the upper classes were opposed to the education of rural laborers because it constituted a tax burden. Victor Clark also noted that the upper class experienced political fears: "they foresee that an educated rural working population, possessed of the suffrage, will ultimately obtain control of the government; and in part is attributable to the fundamental conviction that uneducated rural population may not be willing to devote itself to the crude and simple tasks of the unskilled agricultural laborer." (Clark 78). Problems in the language in which the classes were taught, lack of teachers interested in becoming established in rural areas, and lack of adequate financial support also contributed to the already deteriorating situation of the education in Puerto Rico by the early 1930s. See Aida Negrón de Montilla, *Americanization in Puerto Rico and the Public School System, 1900-1930* (Río Piedras: Puerto Rico Editorial Edil, 1970) and José Osuna, *A History of Education in Puerto Rico* (New York: Arno Press, 1975).
12. Clark, 37.
13. Quintero Rivera, *Conflictos de clase y política en Puerto Rico,* 70. I am making reference to Ángel Quintero's Rivera "triangle theory" that points to the class and political tensions between a displaced *hacendado* class, the emergence of a strong working class and the U.S. corporate and political interests.

14. Quintero, 148-150.
15. Dietz, 113-115.
16. Quintero, 153.
17. Bolívar Pagán, *Historia de los partidos políticos en Puerto Rico* (San Juan: Librería Campos, 1959), 9-12.
18. Pagán, 9-12.
19. Pagán, 40-41. Both political organizations believed in the ultimate admission of Puerto Rico as a state of the Union as a solution to the political status of the island, but for very different reasons. The Socialists saw the United States as the real champion of labor class rights, and the Republicans, formed by the local industrial and agrarian interests and professionals, looked to statehood to preserve their economic and political interests.
20. Arturo Morales Carrión, *Puerto Rico a Political and Cultural History*, (New York: W.W. Norton & Company, 1983), 226.
21. For instance, Republican Juán Serrallés in the sugar industry and María Arcelay in the garment industry were senators elected by the Coalition.
22. Gervasio García and Ángel Quintero, *Desafío y solidaridad: breve historia sobre el movimiento obrero en Puerto Rico* (Río Piedras: Ediciones Huracán, 1986), 101-125.
23. Quintero, 127.
24. Blanca Silvestrini, *Los trabajadores puertorriqueños y el Partido Socialista* (Río Piedras: Editorial de la Universidad de Puerto Rico, 1979), 121-146.
25. Carmelo Rosario Natal, *La juventud de Luis Muñoz Marín* (Río Piedras: Editorial Edil, 1989), 1-179.
26. Luis Muñoz Marín, *Memorias* (San Juan: Universidad Interamericana, 1982), 107.
27. Marisa Rosado, *Las llamas de la aurora: Un acercamiento a la biografía de Pedro Albizu Campos* (República Dominicana: Editorial Corripio, 1991), 59.
28. Pagán, 329-331.
29. In Oct 1935, four members of the Nationalist Party were shot to death by members of the insular police in Río Piedras. Months later, on Feb 23, 1936, two members of the Nationalist Party, Hiram Rosado and Elías Beauchamp, assassinated the Chief of the Puerto Rico Police Department, Colonel Elisha Riggs, in retaliation of the party members killed in Río Piedras. The two Nationalists that perpetrated the assassination of Riggs were shot to death in the headquarters of the police in San Juan. Perhaps the culmination of this wave of violence was the Ponce Massacre of Mar 23, 1937. During a peaceful manifestation of Nationalist Party members in the southern town of Ponce police opened fire upon the manifestation, killing 19 people (including two policemen) and wounding 100.
30. Rosado, 142.

31. The judicial process against Albizu Campos and other members of the Nationalist Party was plagued with discrepancies and problems. On Apr 19, 1936, the seven Puerto Rican members of the jury voted against five Americans for the absolution of all the charges against the Nationalists. As a result, a new judicial process was assigned on Jul 27, 1936. This time the composition of the jury was changed to 10 American and two Puerto Ricans. By Jul 31, 1936, Albizu and his fellow party members were declared guilty as charged.
32. Historian Ángel Ferrao suggests an alternative perspective about Albizu Campos and the presence of the Nationalist Party in Puerto Rico during the 1930s. According to Ferrao, the nationalist discourse proposed an economic model that benefited the native class of *hacendados* displaced by American corporate capital in 1898. Ferrao argues that this *hacendado* class was unable to convince the working class to join forces with the Nationalist Party, impeding a potential alliance between these two political forces. See Luis A. Ferrao, *Pedro Albizu Campos y el nacionalismo Puertorriqueño* (Río Piedras: Editorial Edil, 1990), 125-172.
33. Tugwell, 12.
34. According to Tugwell, the Department of State favored Cuban sugar producers when Congress approved a restriction on sugar production as a result of the AAA policies. Many Puerto Rican sugar producers resented such preference by the State department.
35. Clark, ix.
36. Theodore Roosevelt, Jr., *Colonial Policies of the United States* (New York: Doubleday & Company, 1937), 116-117.
37. Roosevelt, 119.
38. Roosevelt, 202.
39. By 1935, both agencies were declared illegal by the United States Supreme Court. See Basil Rauch, *The History of the New Deal* (New York: Capricorn Books, 1963), 191-222.
40. Memorandum for the Secretary of War from Creed F. Cox, Oct 20, 1933. "Agricultural Adjustment Administration and Federal Farm Board", RG 350, National Archives, Washington, D.C.
41. Many Puerto Ricans feared that the increase in the prices of basic foodstuffs would condemn thousands to hunger. As explained by the Puerto Rican lawyer Ruiz de Valle in a letter to President Roosevelt: "The reason what I'm writing to you is the outrageous and incredible rise in the products of basic necessity. In the last years, our people have not had too much to eat but at least they have had something because of the low prices of the food. The rise in the prices will force us to the very limits of our acquisitive power." Letter From Jose Ruiz to Governor Beverly, Mar 11, 1933, Archivo Fortaleza AGPR, San Juan, Puerto Rico.
42. Letter from R. Carrión to Secretary Dern, May 11, 1934, Bureau of Insular

Affairs, RG 350, National Archives, Washington, D.C. According to Carrión, after the approval of the AAA, Puerto Ricans had to pay $20 million more for articles of primary necessity than 10 years earlier.
43. Most necessary foodstuffs were imported by Puerto Rico because of the negative impact of the sugar industries on subsistence agriculture.
44. Letter from Governor Robert Gore to General Parker Chief, the Bureau of Insular affairs, Aug. 3, 1933, RG 350, National Archives, Washington, D.C.
45. Letter from Homer S. Cummings to President Roosevelt, Sept. 29, 1933, FDR Official Papers Appointments 400 FDR Library, Hyde Park New York.
46. "El presidente de la cámara de comercio de Puerto Rico analiza la ley de Ajuste Agrícola y expresa su opinión al efecto," *El Mundo,* Dec 5, 1933, 1.
47. Ibid., 1.
48. "Documento sometido por la Asociación de Industriales con respecto a la aplicación de la ley de ajuste agrícola en Puerto Rico," *El Mundo,* Nov 29, 1933, 1.
49. A bill to include sugar beets and sugar cane as basic agricultural commodities under the Agricultural Adjustment Act and for other purposes Feb 12, 1934, Bureau of Insular Affairs, RG 350, National Archives, Washington, D.C.
50. Thomas Mathews, *Puerto Rican Politics and the New Deal* (Gainesville: University of Florida Press, 1960), 131-135. The case of Cuba presents some particularities. As a result of the political instability caused by the fall of the Cuban President Gerardo Machado and the rise of Fulgencio Batista to power, the U.S. was reluctant to recognize the government of the latter. The United States, fearing the fall of the importation of U.S. products by the Cubans eased the importation tax on Cuban sugar to preserve the profits of that market. Puerto Rican producers felt betrayed by such policies arguing that as U.S. citizens, they deserved preference in the sugar markets.
51. Letter from Prudencio Rivera Martínez to the Advisory committee of the Secretary of Agriculture, May 9, 1934, Bureau of Insular Affairs, National Archives, RG 350, Washington, D.C.
52. According to Martínez and Alonso, 125,000 workers in Puerto Rico were engaged in sugar cane cultivation. Memorandum from Prudencio Rivera Martínez and Rafael Alonso to the Policy Committee Advisory to the Secretary of Agriculture, May 9, 1934, RG 350, National Archives, Washington, D.C.
53. Ibid., 2-3.
54. Ibid.
55. Letter from Jorge Bird Arias to Governor Blanton Winship, Jun 2, 1934,

RG 350, National Archives, Washington, D.C.
56. Letter from José L. Pesquera of the Farmers Association of Puerto Rico to Secretary of the War Department George Dern, Apr 24, 1934 RG 350, National Archives, Washington, D.C.
57. The point argued by Winship referred to the destruction of the sugar cane fields caused by hurricanes *San Felipe* in 1928 and *San Ciprián* in 1932. These hurricanes affected the production of sugar for the next two years. Winship's concern resided in the possibility that the sugar quota assigned to Puerto Rico could not be met due to the impact of these hurricanes on the sugar crop.
58. Cablegram from Governor Winship to the Department of War, Apr 23, 1934, RG 350, National Archives, Washington, D.C.
59. Ibid.
60. "Aboy Benítez dice que si se nos excluyese de la ley de Ajustes Agrarios sería crítica la situación del comercio y pequeñas industrias," *El Mundo*, Dec, 4 1933, 1. In the final version of the Act, the Puerto Rican quota was trimmed to 803,000.
61. Ibid.
62. Mathews, 122-126. In the long term, an agreement was reached in the garment industries with the establishment of a differential salary that meant that workers were paid less than in the States, in order to preserve the very existence of this industry in Puerto Rico.
63. In a letter to Stephen Early, Boaz Long (later appointed as Ambassador to Colombia) wrote about the experiences he had, with strikes on the docks, with sugar cane workers, and with the San Juan chauffeurs as a results of a rise in price in gasoline just a few days after his arrival. He was particularly impressed with the situation in the sugar cane strike: "for some days there has been a strike at one of the largest sugar mills, which look serious. If unsettled it might spread and end in tragic losses to the labor of this island. Every effort is being made to settle it." Letter from Boaz Long Administrator of the NRA in Puerto Rico to Stephen Early, Jan 5, 1934, FDR official papers appointments 400 FDR Library Hyde Park, New York.
64. "La Asociación de Industriales se dirige al General Johnson," *El Mundo*, Jul 10, 1933, 1.
65. Ibid.
66. "El asunto de los códigos industriales será discutido," *El Mundo*, Jul 20, 1933, 1.
67. For a study about the implementation of the FLSA in Puerto Rico, see Manuel R. Rodríguez, *La reforma liberal en el contexto colonial: El Nuevo Trato y el Fair Labor Standard Act en Puerto Rico, 1938-1940* MA Thesis, University of Puerto Rico, 1996.
68. Much of the funding of New Deal programs included the NRA and AAA where directed to the PRERA offices.

CHAPTER 2

From Emergency Relief to Development: The Emergence of the Puerto Rico Emergency Relief Administration

The PRERA as a Development Project

By 1933 the colonial model established by the United States in Puerto Rico in 1898 had begun to show signs of deterioration. Moreover, political unrest represented in the activities of the Nationalist Party arose throughout the island questioning the legitimacy of the U.S. presence in Puerto Rico. The arrival of the Great Depression also added hardships and widespread misery to the already deteriorated living conditions of thousands of Puerto Ricans. In the midst of all these hectic changes, the first New Deal reforms began to arrive by mid-1933. As explained in chapter one, Puerto Rican and U.S. scholarship both agree that the extension of the New Deal policies to Puerto Rico and the implementation of the PRERA programs constituted limited policies subordinated to political opportunism and that excessive bureaucratic control did little to confront the serious economic and social problems experienced on the island by the 1930s. These historiographical narratives tend to obscure other possibilities that concede that the PRERA had a more profound and decisive impact in its attempt to construct a new political relationship between Puerto Rico and the United States.

I argue that the PRERA embodied in its diverse programs a well-articulated discursive of modernity that operated on a cultural and discourse level on the Puerto Rican society of the 1930s. This perspective escapes the traditional historiography that privileges the political events that affected this New Deal agency and its performance on the island. Thus, this book provides an alternative approach to such perspectives by demonstrating how the management and implementation of the modern discourse contained in the PRERA policies allowed the United States to re-think the parameters of its colonial regime in Puerto Rico. Thus the PRERA, far more than being a short-term policy of emergency help a strategy of imperial domination, or an initiative of the Roosevelt administration to provide temporary relief to a needy territorial possession on the verge of economic disaster, constituted a carefully crafted project of development that embodied a technology of domination over the colonial subjects, allowing the United States to establish new principles of governing in Puerto Rico during the 1930s.

This chapter will examine the United States as a regime of representation, the first steps in the implementation of a New Deal order on the island, and the complex bureaucratic structure of the PRERA. First, this chapter will analyze the establishment of such a regime of representation prior to the establishment of the PRERA in Puerto Rico. In order to guarantee the success of the development initiatives brought by the PRERA, U.S. authorities who were assigned to the island had to develop a powerful discourse of modernity in order to convince broad sectors of Puerto Rican society to accept these projects as a chance to transform their daily lives and material conditions. Second, in an effort to understand the transformation of the PRERA in the context of a potential development project, it is then necessary to map out the initial steps of other New Deal programs, the Agricultural Adjustment Act (AAA), and National Recovery Administration (NRA). The efforts to establish these programs on the island can provide us with a point of departure necessary to understand the early origins of the PRERA. Third, in order to provide a context in which to situate the PRERA, this section will focus on the early emergence of the agency and its complex bureaucratic structures. The complex and extensive organization of its programs demonstrated that it was more than an emergency relief agency. Its bureaucratic organization sought to reach almost every aspect of Puerto Rican society. The organizational structure of the PRERA reflected the basis of the development project envisioned by the agency and the Roosevelt administration. The organizational structure of these bureaucratic units reflect the commitment of the Americans and Puerto Ricans in charge of the PRERA to utilize the New Deal programs to articulate a modernizing project for the social and economic development of Puerto Rico using the New Deal in the initial years of the 1930s.

The Politics of Representation

In the early stages of the implementation of the New Deal, Americans and the elite sectors of Puerto Rican society sought in its initiatives an opportunity to bring progress and modernity to a struggling territorial possession. In order to accomplish such objectives, U.S. metropolitan authorities, with the close cooperation of Puerto Rican professional sectors, had to create an effective representation of the desperate socio–economic conditions of Puerto Rico prior to the establishment of the PRERA. This process of the representation of poverty was not exclusive to the Puerto Rican situation and has been studied by other scholars in Latin America. Colombian anthropologist Arturo Escobar has analyzed the process in which the concept of poverty has been managed by the West in an attempt to "sell" a particular model of development in an attempt to exercise political power upon underdeveloped nations. Escobar called this process a regime of representation; a place for encountering where identities are constructed. Escobar's analysis proposes that any regime of representation has to be constituted by three elements:

> "The forms of knowledge that refer to it and through which it comes into being and are elaborated into objects, concepts, theories, and the like; a system of power that regulates its practice; and the forms of subjectivity by this discourse, those through which people come to recognize themselves as developed or underdeveloped."[1]

Escobar's definition of the regime of representation is important to understand the origins of the development rationale behind the PRERA policies. A new set of theories and practices and regulative institutions were seen by PRERA officials as necessary in order to improve the detrimental conditions of Puerto Rico. The agency envisioned for that task was the PRERA. Crucial to the representation of the PRERA as a development initiative was the attempt to establish, among the island inhabitants, a difference between those who were developed undeveloped. In the case of 1930s Puerto Rico, a representation of poverty and misery was crucial to make Puerto Ricans aware of the necessity of establishing the development initiatives offered by the United States in an attempt to improve their material conditions.

This idea of a regime of representation can certainly be applied to Puerto Rico as a preamble for the establishment of the PRERA development programs. Prior and during the implementation of the PRERA, U.S. investigators were sent to the island in an effort to create a messianic image of the New Deal initiatives proposed by the United States. The articulation of this regime of representation also contributed to convince Puerto Ricans, regardless of class extraction, as to the necessity of a development initiative to "save" the island from the chaos caused by the Depression and also to stop any potential social dissatisfaction with the U.S. colonial rule over Puerto Rico. This regime of representation operated at a discursive level, providing the necessity, demand, acceptance, and legitimization of the PRERA presence by the Puerto Ricans. [2] The representation of the PRERA as a development project that would provide prosperity to Puerto Rico would ease and expand the political domination of the United States over the island. Thus, the PRERA represented a depository of the technical and organizational knowledge, an institution able to transform the economic calamities of a poor Caribbean territory.

In addition the PRERA transformed the ways in which thousands of Puerto Ricans perceived the presence of the U.S. government in the island. After thirty-two years of a one-crop economy that sent into abject misery thousands of Puerto Rican families, the PRERA offered a way to improve their material conditions. It is no wonder then how the examination of the documents that contained the particular views of the people depicted the PRERA as an institution that had considerable and positive impact in their lives. The once far-off and indifferent metropolitan state suddenly demonstrated concern about their citizens in the Caribbean. Soon progress was identified with the intervention of the metropolitan state extending the regulative power of the United States and making its colonial presence more tolerable to Puerto Ricans.

The articulation of this regime of representation was possible thanks to the active participation of the U.S. New Deal officials assigned to the island and a local bureaucracy committed to the modernity promised by the PRERA. The discourses produced from the visits, examinations, writing reviews field trips, personal documents, and publications by New Dealers such as Rexford Tugwell, Alan Johnstone, and Robert Watson were seminal in helping us to understand how a regime of representation was able to first shape opinion and later establish the bases of the PRERA's development project. The arguments of these New Deal officials significantly contributed to the construction of a harsh image of the island, whose only way to overcome its precarious social and economic conditions depended on the scientifically constructed and modern programs brought by the PRERA.

Among the Americans who visited Puerto Rico in the early 1930s was Robert Watson. Watson was an examiner from the FERA sent to Puerto Rico by Harry Hopkins, to report the economic and social conditions of the island.[3] Watson pointed out that the Depression hit the sugar industry hard in Puerto Rico because the island's economy dependency on this sector. He was impressed by the high volume in the production of sugar and the imports of foodstuffs, the high rate of unemployment, and the absence of gardens or land plots to supplement the peasant diet. One of Watson's most revealing comments were about the large number of blacks in Puerto Rico. Watson was clearly alarmed because of the proportion between blacks and whites in the island:

> "The proportion of black and white in the island is unknown in Puerto Rico, the census data to the contrary notwithstanding. It is generally understood that most white families, with a residence of over a generation in Puerto Rico, have a black strain in their family lives, more or less pronounced; estimates of the proportion vary from two thirds to 95 percent black. Many of the white race, attributing their ancestry to

the Spanish nationality and with distinct Latin American complexion, are in reality very largely Negro. These factors have contributed very largely to the lax social standards, which are ever present on the island."[4]

Watson's analysis about the racial composition of the average Puerto Rican clearly demonstrates his racial bias. Even the white elite are not saved from Watson's racial contempt. According to this U.S. bureaucrat, the white inhabitants of the island were "stained" with black blood in their veins. According to Watson, the Depression or the colonial policies implemented in the island since 1898 were not valid reasons to explain its chronic socio-economic problems. Instead, the racial composition of Puerto Ricans is the cause of "lax social standards" as the origin of its social problems. According to Watson:

"Family customs and traditions of Puerto Rico are distinctly unique. The husband of the family may live with his wife for several years and very suddenly break off the family obligation, and start another family with no legal or moral responsibility for the first family, even throughout there may be five or six children. This family situation has contributed largely to the social and economic difficulties of the island, and has a definite bearing on the administration of relief, because it is often very difficult to check names in the listing of applicants for relief in order to be sure there is no duplication."[5]

For Watson, the alarming numbers of births and the low mortality rates represented a lethal combination that contributed to the fragmentary nature of the typical Puerto Rican family. Following the logic of his analysis, all Puerto Rican families lived a precarious existence with a father who continuously deserts his obligations and undermines the society's familial institutions. As Watson suggested, the absence of a social commitment or moral considerations makes virtually impossible the implementation of the relief administration to provide assistance for the needy. The lack of "solid family values" and racial diversity constituted the cause of the detrimental social and economic conditions of Puerto Ricans. In other words, Puerto Ricans were the ones responsible of their own fate. Even the social order that the metropolitan state tried to implement in the island throughout the emergency relief administration was threatened by the lack of family planning. These moral and racial problems had to be resolved by the "civilized" intervention of the United States and the implementation of modern programs that would guarantee progress and better living conditions. Watson's solutions for Puerto Rico relied in the extension of the reconstruction programs in the areas of housing, industry, agriculture, and health programs.[6] In sum, Watson represented the island as a place in which race and moral decay constituted the basis of most of Puerto Rico's problems.

Alan Johnston, field representative of the Federal Emergency Relief administration (FERA) echoed the representational model articulated by Watson.[7] In his description of the islands conditions Johnstone comments on the agricultural nature of the island and the backwardness of its industries. Similar to other investigators, Johnstone concluded that the only profitable industry in the island was sugar, controlled by absentee landlords. Nonetheless, Johnstone recognized that the island has some peculiarities that make more complex the implementation of an emergency help program. Referring to Puerto Ricans he argued:

> "that this people are alike to the Latin peoples of the world, and their mode of living and reactions are in many respects unlike those of the people of the continental United States leaves it is, therefore, impossible and impracticable to inaugurate a system of social work and relief administration of the exact pattern as that which prevails in the states."[8]

As Watson, Johnstone argues that because Puerto Rican and Latin American people were different and had "living conditions and reactions" was not possible to implement a federal aid system similar to the one existing in the United States. The metropolitan state reserved for itself the right to authorize or condemn the institutional policies to be implemented upon the people under their political domination. Puerto Rican and Latin American individuals were represented as backward individuals because they were "different" to the people in the

United States. Therefore, special institutions had to be created to deal with these populations in an effort to guide them in the ways of a modern, progressive and civilized country. In the context of the regime of representation proposed by Escobar, Johnstone portrayed the United States as the arbiter able to authorize and legitimize the institutions that are "good or bad" for the welfare of Puerto Ricans. Thus, Johnstone represented the people of the island as infantile individuals who needed the guidance of the metropolitan state to bring order and prosperity to their country.

The representation of Puerto Ricans as those who needed guidance and the United States as the institution that would dictate what was correct or not to their citizens in the Caribbean also echoed by Rexford Tugwell as well. In the mid 1930s, Tugwell was commissioned by President Roosevelt to conduct a study about the possibilities of the establishment of a colonial tropical policy for the U.S. Caribbean possessions. For Roosevelt and Tugwell, the tropics became the ultimate arena in which proved the virtues of the American exceptionalism. The articulation of such policy was important to implement all the knowledge necessary to govern and exercise economic domination over tropical possessions. One of the most important aspects of Tugwell was is to recognize the failure of previous colonial polices applied on tropical possessions. In his report to President Roosevelt, Tugwell recognizes the failure of the colonial model established by the United States in 1898:

> "We are likely to try to play lady bountiful against the unanswerable bounty of the tropics and to attempt to Americanize people who are entirely different from North Americans. However, we can certainly make a start by ending our own exploitation of tropical inexperience and helplessness. We should direct our policy in the interest of encouraging a more effective and fuller use of the resources; obtaining a more equitable distribution of the income from the resources; and creating financial and economic reserves with which to cushion shocks as hurricanes, earthquakes, and economic depressions. It is probable that effective first steps in this directions will have to assume the form of reorgan-

izing and redirecting the various institutions and services (credit facilities, use of federal funds, and control of the resources of the island in general, for example) as most of these inhabitants of these regions have shown themselves reluctant to raise their individual standards of consumption above the point necessary to support life with a minimum effort."[9]

Arguing that the United States had to put an end to its own exploitation on the tropics, Tugwell recognized the failure of the Americanization project established in 1898. He clearly argued that Puerto Ricans were different form North Americans. Consequently, the United States had the responsibility to provide a new economic model based on healthy credit and financial institutions and assume a "rational" control of the island resources. Based on a Keynesian rational, Tugwell assumed that such changes in the Puerto Rican economy would arouse a rate of consumption necessary to "support life with a minimum effort".

The "enlightened" approach for a policy in the tropics did not exclude Tugwell from creating an "uncivilized" representation of Puerto Ricans. According to Tugwell, Puerto Ricans loved their way of life and were not interested in bringing substantial changes to it. As Tugwell explained:

"It is useless and stupid to attempt to do anything for such people without being positive that it is what they really want. Increased wages in the centrals (sugar refineries) have, in many cases, simply led to the men working half time, as a family can be supported on with three or four dollars a week. Increased wages in the needle industry have simply led to a higher birth rate. Their owners are using model houses for tobacco barns. Families removed from the unsanitary huts in the mangrove swamps and settled on subsistence homesteads have promptly returned to the mangrove swamps. The general belief is that the Puerto Ricans would rather have more children than increase their standard of living. Here is a condition, which calls for very slow and wise action on our part rather than indulgence in preconceived charities."[10]

Tugwell's solution for this situation was "to adequate ourselves to the habits and desire of the Puerto Ricans".[11] According to the New Dealers previously mentioned and Tugwell, the contempt of Puerto Ricans toward family values, good housing, and a Protestant work ethic made them unworthy and unprepared to assume the modernity and the progress brought by the United States. Their cultural backwardness constituted an obstacle for progress and prosperity. As an alternative, Tugwell proposed a new and interesting policy; throughout the extension of the New Deal programs to Puerto Rico:

> "For the lesson of the tropics is the object of the New Deal: a more abundant life. If we, by social control of wealth can confer upon our people a similar accessibility to wealth to that which is enjoyed by the inhabitants of these islands, we may re-establish a civilization in which women do not fear to bear children and men do not hesitate to undertake family responsibilities. Without that our race is doomed to degeneration and decay."[12]

The Tugwellian idea of the New Deal in Puerto Rico was conceived as strategy to vindicate the awkward colonial policies of the United States toward Puerto Rico after decades of U.S. political domination. For the first time since 1898, a U.S. official recognized that the United States had the responsibility to provide the same access of wealth to Puerto Ricans as the one enjoyed by "our people," i.e. continental Americans. According to Tugwell, the failure of such responsibility would lead to the eventual degeneration and decay of the U.S. civilization, a devastating blow to the discourse of American exceptionalism. Tugwell's New Deal project also embodied the premises of a crusade to rescue Puerto Rican from their moral backwardness. The application of the messianic policies of the New Deal would contribute to vanish the fear of the Puerto Rican women to bear children and taught Puerto Rican men to assume their familiar responsibility. By this means the New Deal policies transcended their economic goals and became the arbiter of morality and good customs throughout the implementation of their development programs.

The model of representation previously examined is correct in its assessment about the difficult economic conditions experienced in the island in the early 1930s. The representation models presented by Watson, Johnstone and Tugwell are beyond simple economic considerations. For Watson and Johnstone, racial and moral issues contributed in the articulation of a representation model about Puerto Ricans as individuals responsible for their own economic and social problems. For them, Puerto Ricans were irresponsible creatures condemned by racial heritage and strange family practices. Despite Tugwell's sharing of this discriminatory representation about Puerto Ricans, he was able to propose a new approach to the problem. This approach was based on the implementation of an enlightened colonialism that demonstrated tolerance toward the Puerto Rican culture and at the same time assumed the responsibility to them as "our citizens of the Caribbean." In any case, the U.S. government was represented as an omnipotent institution with the authority to determine what is right or wrong for their citizens in the Caribbean.

In summary, Puerto Ricans on the eve of the implementation of the PRERA programs were portrayed as needy creatures waiting for the benefits of an enlightened state to bring progress and modernity in an effort to transcend their racial and moral decay. Once the islanders learned about the "benefits" of progress and modernity, they would be ready to occupy their place in the civilized world. As we will see in the next chapters, the PRERA would provide an opportunity to "rescue" Puerto Ricans of their economic and social backwardness and at the same time prove the "effectiveness" of the metropolitan state in the welfare of its tropical possessions.

The Bureaucracy of Development

On August 19, 1933, the PRERA was established as an operative extension of the FERA in Puerto Rico.[13] From the very beginning, James Bourne, the administrator of the newly formed agency, and most Washington New Dealers, envisioned the PRERA as a bureaucratic unit that would provide the island with not only work and food relief, but also with a comprehensive and feasible plan of development. The administrator's wife, Dorothy Bourne, shared that perspective, probably as a result of her experience as director of the local government program of social work.[14] The couple also had strong ties with the Roosevelts, a fact that contributed to the president being well informed of the new events concerning the agency.[15] As Tugwell argued in his report about the establishment of a tropical policy, the Bournes considered the application of this plan as an obligation towards their citizens in the Caribbean:

> "We assumed an obligation in 1898. In 1917, when we gave citizenship to Puerto Ricans this obligation was confirmed. If this means anything it means the establishment of American ideals and standards in education, in health and equal opportunities."[16]

The Bournes believed that the colonial policies implemented by the United States in Puerto Rico were in opposition to the ideals that made the U.S. exceptional among other colonial nations. Appealing to the fact that the United States had an obligation to the island and its citizens, the Bournes justified the application of a complete and well-articulated program able to demonstrate that the "American ideals" were able to establish an exceptional model of developmental colonialism. By December 6, 1933, they proposed to the War Department a "constructive plan" for the rehabilitation of Puerto Rico.[17]

The plan, later called the PRERA, covered the areas of economy, health, education, taxation, labor housing, slum clearance, population, publicity, and even politics. Accordingly, the departments that constituted the PRERA were created along the core bureaucratic structures of the agency consisted of the following departments: Bureau of Social Service, Engineering Division, Division of Agriculture, and the Education Division. The second category offered logistical support to these core bureaucratic units. This category consisted of the Bureau of Accounts, the Personnel Division, and the Publicity and Safety Departments. The third category supported the other two with the data necessary to pinpoint the necessities of the agency operations and the establishment of an empirical rationale for future development projects. This category included the Research Bureau of Accounts and the Bureau of Statistics.

The agency in which the rest of the operational systems of the

PRERA were based was the Bureau of Social Service.[18] The tasks performed by the Bureau were divided into two areas: first, provide direct help to individuals, and second, recommend people eligible to participate in the public works programs sponsored by the Civil Works Administration (CWA) or Civilian Conservation Corps (CCC) or Public Works Administration (PWA).[19] Most of the personnel working under the Social Work Division did not possess a university degree in social work at the time the division started to operate in Puerto Rico. As a result, personnel with no university studies in the field were allowed to work as "aides," especially in investigation and fieldwork.[20] The standard procedure to process applicants consisted of completing an application requesting services from the division in their local town.[21] Once this step was completed, the local office of the division set a date for a home visit by two aides to evaluate the conditions of the person or family that requested help. The evaluation of these social workers determined if the family or person would be granted alimentary relief or assigned to public work if availability permitted. The Social Work Division constituted an agency of resources to the needy sectors of the island population. The complex operation of the Social Service Division evidences the intricate bureaucratic net established by the PRERA on the island. Far from constituting a distant institution, the Social Service Division represented a complex bureaucratic order with the purpose of examining, classifying, and designating the place of individuals within society. The presence of this division, as part of the PRERA's programs, suggests that the New Deal authorities reserved for itself the responsibility to place individuals within the occupational niches available in the island's job market and assign emergency help to the ones who needed it. This new image of the "metropolitan welfare state" certainly was the precedent in which the social service programs of the following decades were conceived to provide social services in urban and rural areas throughout the island.

The Engineering (or Work) Division was another of the core agencies that made up the PRERA. Its agenda was directed at the development of the island's infrastructure, such as the construction of bridges, roads, sanitary systems and dikes and the filling of lowlands.[22] In order to accomplish such a goal, the Work Division of the PRERA had the responsibility to distribute, organize, and determine the different engineering projects to be built on the island. Most of the funding assigned to the engineer division came from other New Deal agencies such as the CWA, PWA, and other New Deal agencies.[23] The people who worked on the projects were chosen from lists provided by the Bureau of Social Work, based on the level of expertise and academic preparation required by the different constructions projects. From August 1933 to August, 1934, the Work Division completed its projects with funds from the CWA. Among the projects completed with CWA funds were the construction and reparation of bridges, insular and federal roads, public buildings such as schools and hospitals, athletic fields and sewer disposal facilities. CWA funds also fought and isolated malaria, along with other disease sources like stagnant water were eradicated. The works-engineering programs not only provided jobs for unemployed workers, their roads, bridges and sanitary facilities also constituted a monument for the new regime of progress that the PRERA intended to establish in the island. In the worst days of the Depression such projects demonstrated to thousands of Puerto Ricans the new image of a once-distant metropolitan state. The impact of these projects on the island's infrastructure would influence the traditional perspective in which Puerto Ricans conceived the federal institutions while at the same time constituted a reminder of the possibilities to change their material conditions.

The Educational Division was considered one of the pivotal offices of the PRERA. At the moment when the Educational Division started to function, the Puerto Rican Department of Education was in the midst of one of its worst crises since the arrival of the Americans in 1898. About 370,000 children were not receiving education, the supervising system needed serious readjustments, and a grading system was needed to evaluate student performance and academic advancement. The insular Department of Education did not have enough resources to cover such areas.[24] This situation compelled the Educational Division of the PRERA to complement the efforts of the local Educational Department to confront the serious problems of education of Puerto Rico. In its initial stages the agency concentrated its efforts on the construction of schools and the employment of teachers. For these purposes, the division also helped to provide statistical data to recruit and determine where to assign teachers specialized in fields of interest such as home economic teachers, teachers for the bureau of extension and examination, athletic instructors, school directors, day care teachers, and urban teachers.[25] An aggressive plan to expand the physical facilities of the educational system was also proposed.[26] The division sponsored research projects designed to improve and develop reading and writing skills among the island's students in coordination with the insular Department of Education, including the establishment of nursery schools and adult education programs for people who did not write or read.[27] Due to the enormous amount of work, the Educational Division was supported by a vast array of support and logistical offices within its own jurisdiction: Office of Statistics, Bureau of Publications, and a Supervision Division. These offices provided the division with an empirical base on which to design and execute its programs and initiatives.[28] The educational division projects represented one of the pivotal divisions of the PRERA. Besides its contribution in terms of the physical expansion of the local educational system, the educational division had the responsibility of transmitting the modernizing discourses embodied in the PRERA programs. Their nurseries, adult education and vocational programs helped facilitate the insertion of thousands of people in the local working force.

The Agriculture Division completed the core agencies that constituted the PRERA. Organized in February, 1934, this agency was in charge of resolving the serious problems facing Puerto Rico whose agricultural assets relied exclusively on a cash-crop economy. Accordingly, its main objective was to design programs for the purpose of developing subsistence crops to complement the peasant diet and open to new spaces to agricultural business.[29] One of the first problems attacked by this division was the need to deal with the excessive importation of basic foodstuffs to the island. For this purpose, the Agricultural Division organized an extensive program of home gardens in which "poor classes" would be able to plant their own food without depending on importation.[30] Another project proposed by the agricultural division was devoted to the production of community gardens, home canning of farm products, cooperative exchanges, and cotton production.[31] The establishment of the agricultural division of the PRERA illustrates the many contradictory situations created by colonialism. For decades the United States was reluctant to enforce the limitation of land devoted to the cultivation of sugar and privileged the importation of basic foodstuffs to the island. By the 1930s, PRERA planners realized that this situation were lethal for the material conditions of the average Puerto Rican. The rationale behind the activities of the agricultural division was designed to face this problem. This division sponsored an ambitious plan for the developing of subsistence crops in an effort to curb the damaging effects of a one-crop economy. Notwithstanding, their efforts were limited because their incapacity to transform the institutional policies that did not allow the limitation of land for the cultivation of sugar.

Other divisions were created in order to provide logistical support to the diverse PRERA projects. Among those units are the Bureau of Accounts, the Personnel Division, and the Publicity and Safety Departments. The Bureau of Accounts had the difficult job of coordinating the complex financial transactions between the funds allocated by U.S. government and Puerto Rico.[32] The Accounting Department was crucial to the funding operations of the PRERA because of the complexity of the process and the added fact that all the funds coming from federal sources were deposited into the insular government treasury. Because of these particular circumstances, the PRERA appointed two of its accounting officials to speed up the payroll process of the different PRERA divisions, bureaus and departments. The Department of Personnel was in charge of selecting and distributing the applications for jobs according to the social work department criteria. One of the most interesting aspects of this unit was its great interest in jobs in the white collar sector. As of October 31, 1934, 8,300 applications were received for the following jobs: architects, bookkeepers, accountants, chemists, clerks, doctors, engineers, executives, foremen, health units, pharmacists, nurses, photographers, printers, inspectors of gasoline, typists, teachers, publicity, watchmen, etc.[33] The impact of the PRERA, especially in the island's occupational field was enormous. By 1930, the Puerto Rican labor force was constituted of approximately 500,000 members, of this total, the local government employed 11,500.[34] By August of 1934, a total of 5,000 persons were employed by the PRERA in white-collar positions.[35] That means that the PRERA significantly contributed to the expansion of the island bureaucracy as a result of the implementation of its development programs. As a result, the government became in one of the largest employers in the island, contributing to curb the unemployment rate during that period.³⁶

The Safety Division of the PRERA also formed part of this logistical category. Organized on January 15, 1934, this unit was in charge of work protection regulations and health for the PRERA personnel throughout its bureaus and divisions. This division was also responsible for the distribution of printed material about safety procedures, the training of first aid through National Red Cross courses, and the coordination of workmen compensation with insular government authorities.³⁷ The Publicity Division was responsible for the distribution of information about the PRERA activities and projects throughout the island. Among the resources created for such a task were the weekly publication of the PRERA's newspaper, *La Rehabilitación,* the distribution and coordination of programs and recent news about the progress of the PRERA projects in local newspapers and on radio, and even the production of a short film about the PRERA.³⁸

Other bureaucratic units of the PRERA were established to support the operation of the key relief units. These divisions provided the research and statistical knowledge by which the operation other bureaucratic units of the PRERA such as agriculture, work relief and education would operate. The PRERA research bureau was one of the bureaucratic units designed for this purpose. According to this division, some of the reasons why the economy of Puerto Rico was in such a deplorable condition was the lack of knowledge about conditions, indifference to local particularities, the inability to comprehend details of competition, and failure to adapt projects to prevailing conditions.

The task of the Research Bureau was to examine the viability of the establishment of new industries and agricultural projects, to investigate the further development of already existing agricultural projects, to analyze the potential of recycling waste programs, and to make tables showing the comparative costs and profits per acre of various crops.³⁹ The Bureau of Statistics was also designed to establish a "knowledge field" to provide reliable statistical information for the establishment and implementation of the different PRERA projects. The statistical knowledge generated by this division constituted the basis of almost all the PRERA programs, especially the social work division. As argued in the 1930s by journalist Carlos Mirabal, "the division of statistics offers to the Social Work Division a solid base that provides the knowledge necessary to point out the problem areas where more help is needed and providing a scientific methodology to improve the social forces."[40]

The establishment of the Research and Statistics Divisions represents another aspect of the new order that the PRERA wished to implement on the island. Scientific and empirical knowledge became the tools that would guarantee the success of the development project envisioned by the PRERA. Once again the U.S. government demonstrated itself as the supreme institution capable of transforming the harsh conditions of Puerto Ricans.

Finally, PRERA officials realized that the success of the program greatly depended on the projection of its organization throughout the island. Consequently, the distribution of the PRERA programs was coordinated through the senatorial districts in which the island was divided. The agency also divided the island into eleven regions, with one office in each town. Each "barrio," or neighborhood of the municipality, had its town head, usually a person in charge of coordinating and presenting community necessities to the local PRERA office. This complex array made possible the modernizing projects of the PRERA, and its progressive discourse penetrated every corner of the island.[41]

Puerto Rican and United States historiography has constantly catalogued the PRERA as a simple New Deal agency devoted to the coordination and distribution of emergency relief. As a result, the presence of the New Deal policies on the island throughout the 1930s has been subordinated by the influence on the Popular Democratic Party (PDP) populist project or its impact on the Puerto Rican working class. The use of the documentary sources to explain the presence of the PRERA on the island has been excessively oriented to these areas, leaving behind numerous aspects that would provide a more integral perspective about the presence of this New Deal agency in Puerto Rico. Among the areas overlooked by traditional historiography are the chaotic circumstances experience by New Deal programs as the NRA and the AAA and the failure to study in a systematic manner complexities of the bureaucratic organization of the PRERA. A revision to the documentary sources about this previously mentioned areas would contribute to clarify the real and profound impact of the PRERA in Puerto

Rican society. Perhaps the most critical of these overlooked areas is the participation of the New Dealers and its importance on the articulation of a regime of representation as a preamble to the establishment of the PRERA as a development project.

The discourse articulated by U.S. officials depicted a chaotic colonial society in which family values, economic infrastructure, and overpopulation were elements that had to be transformed in order to guarantee the success of any development programs on the island. Watson, Hichock, Bourne, Tugwell, and Johnstone were facilitators who convinced not only Washington authorities, but also vast segments of Puerto Rican society about the impact of the Depression and the perils that it posed to the preservation of the colonial regime. Their assessment of the island's condition reflects Escobar's elements that make up a regime of representation. In order to save the island from economic devastation, it was necessary to articulate a set of theories and practices. First, in order to set the foundation for any development project and establish any regulative institution, the establishment of the PRERA was the response for such concerns. This representational strategy also prepared the way to the acceptance of the PRERA by Puerto Rican society. Thus, the PRERA in Puerto Rico was not perceived as a mere emergency relief program, but as well as an integrated and coordinated development plan aimed at transforming the deplorable conditions of the island and reinventing its colonial relationship with the United States. But the success of this attempt relied not only on the implementation by U.S. New Dealers, but also on the ability of Puerto Ricans to adopt and reproduce the discourse of progress and modernity promised by the PRERA.

Notes

1. Arturo Escobar, *Encountering Development: The Making and Unmaking of the Third World* (Princeton: Princeton University Press), 10.
2. A similar process of the representation of the conditions of the "other" is seen in Edward Said's, *Orientalism* (New York: Vintage Books), 1978. Said's analysis has interesting similarities with Escobar's regime of representation. As in Orientalism, development can be seen as a intellectual construction that dictates, defines, authorizes and implements what is or not progress to the people who are suppose to receive their benefits.
3. Memorandum from Robert Watson to Harry Hopkins, file 002 Papers of

Harry Hopkins, Feb 7, 1934, Franklin D. Roosevelt Library, Hyde Park, New York.
4. Ibid, 1.
5. Ibid, 2.
6. Ibid, 13.
7. Report from Alan Johnstone to Harry Hopkins, Aug 17, 1933, 002 Papers of Harry Hopkins, Franklin D. Roosevelt Library, Hyde Park, New York.
8. Ibid.
9. Report on American Tropical Policy from Rexford Tugwell to President Roosevelt, Roosevelt Official Papers, Appointments 400, 1934, Franklin Delano Roosevelt Library, Hyde Park: New York.
10. Ibid., 10.
11. Ibid., 11.
12. Ibid., 19-20.
13. Report from Alan Johnstone to Harry Hopkins, Aug 17, 1933, 002 papers of Harry Hopkins, Franklin D. Roosevelt Library, Hyde Park, New York.
14. "Hablando con Mr. James R. Bourne, jefe de "Puerto Rican Emergency Relief Administration," *El Mundo,* Oct 29, 1933, 1. James Bourne was born on Apr 6, 1897. He graduated from Yale University and served as an artillery officer in World War I. From 1928 to 1929, Bourne worked as administrator of the Brothers Canning Company in Puerto Rico. His wife Dorothy Bourne was the director of the Social Service Office in Puerto Rico.
15. No other program in Puerto Rico had experienced the constant monitoring of an American President since the U.S. took possession of the island in 1898.
16. Letter from James Bourne to Harry Hopkins, Oct 26, 1933, RG 69, FERA Central files State series, March 1933-36, National Archives, Washington, D.C.
17. Report from James Bourne to President Roosevelt "A constructive plan for Puerto Rico", Dec 6, 1933, RG 350, National Archives, Washington, D.C.
18. *PRERA, First Annual Report,* Aug 1933 to Aug 31 1934, Library of Congress, Washington, D.C., 1935, 27-33.
19. This agency operated in Puerto Rico under the auspices of the PRERA. Due to a lack of funding, the CWA only lasted for the initial months of 1934.
20. *PRERA, First Annual Report,* 28. The bureaucratic structure of the Bureau was extremely complex. In a broad sense, the Bureau was constituted of a central office, district office, local office and offices in remote rural areas. A vast amount of aides were responsible for running a good part of the operations of the Social Work Division. Because of the limited number of professional social workers, many of these aides occupied executive posi-

tions as District Directors. This particular circumstance allowed sectors of society (not necessarily coming from an upper-class background) to enter into the white collar occupational realm, allowing them some extent of social mobility. Most of these people could not be considered, as Quintero Rivera argued, as elements of a displaced *hacendado* class, seeking a new social niche in the colonial society. See Ángel Quintero Rivera, *Conflictos de clase y política en Puerto Rico* (Río Piedras: Ediciones Huracán, 1976), 57-59.
21. *PRERA, First Annual Report*, 27-28. Every town throughout the island had a representative of the social work division. The island was divided into 12 districts with five to eight municipalities in each one. Usually the largest municipalities housed the headquarters. The local offices have a town head in charge, which employed the aides to support the operations of the Bureau. The bureau also had sub-offices in distant rural communities.
22. *PRERA, First Annual Report*, Aug 1935-Aug 1934, 168. The projects of the Work Division were deployed throughout 14 districts and classified according to the priority and nature of the project (construction of a bridge, road or sewer et.al.).
23. *PRERA, First Annual Report*, 37-61.
24. *PRERA, First Annual Report*, 404-404. By 1933-34, the Department of Education had no other option but to close 132 rural schools. Of a total of 600,000 students, only 230,000 were taking classes. According to the PRERA, a total of 1,589 urban teachers and 3,600 rural teachers were needed to meet student demand.
25. *PRERA, First Annual Report*, 409-416.
26. The PRERA proposed a plan of $4,000,000 for the construction of new schools during the period of 1934-35.
27. Brief report of the program of activities of the Puerto Rico Emergency Relief Administration, RG 69, FERA central files state series, Mar 1933-36, PR 450 PC 37, entry 10 11-13, National Archives, Washington, D.C.
28. *PRERA, First Annual Report*, 409-410.
29. *PRERA First Annual Report*, 391. The bureaucratic structure of the agency was responsive to those needs. The division had a director and assistant director. It also had a chief general supervisor of agriculture in charge of the programs of community gardens, home gardens, urban gardens, entomology, plant pathology, reports and correspondence.
30. *PRERA, First Annual Report*, 385-395.
31. Ibid.
32. Administrative Set Up of the PRERA, FERA Central Files State Series, Mar 1933-36, RG 69, National Archives Washington, D.C.
33. *PRERA First Annual Report*, 524.
34. James Dietz, *Economic History of Puerto Rico: Institutional Change and Capitalist Development* (Princeton: Princeton University Press, 1986), 177.

35. Ibid.
36. Dietz,136. By 1933, the unemployment rate in Puerto Rico was 24.9 percent.
37. Administrative Set Up of the PRERA, FERA Central Files State Series, Mar 1933-36, RG 69, National Archives Washington, D.C.
38. "Informe general de la división de publicidad de la PRERA," *La Rehabilitación,* (Sep, 1934): 5-7, Library of Congress Washington, D.C.
39. Brief report of the program of activities of the Puerto Rico Emergency Relief Administration, FERA Central Files State Series, Mar 1933-36, RG 69, National Archives, Washington, D.C., 16.
40. "La división de estadísticas y su importancia en la PRERA", *La Rehabilitación* 2 (May 2, 1934), Library of Congress, Washington, D.C.
41. *PRERA, First Annual Report*, 9-13.

CHAPTER 3

The Heralds of Modernity: The Role of Puerto Rican Professionals in the Puerto Rican Relief Administration

Professionalization and the Institutionalization of the PRERA

The development initiatives embodied in the PRERA required the support of a professional sector that was both committed to the progressive discourses embodied in the agency's programs and capable of transforming the material conditions of the island. In addition, this professional sector needed to possess the technical expertise and the ability to reproduce and transmit the knowledge contained in the development initiatives implemented by the PRERA.[1]

Traditional scholarship on the origins and presence of a Puerto Rican professional class in the first three decades of the twentieth century are limited and theological in nature. Sociological and historical narratives limit the participation of Puerto Rican professionals during the 1930s to a displaced *hacendado* class desperately seeking a niche in a new economic order established by the U.S. sugar corporations. The works of sociologists Ángel Quintero and Emilio Pantojas maintain that the bureaucratic structure created by the New Deal programs in Puerto Rico provided a new manner in which the members of the displaced *hacendado* class were able to exercise power and domination over

Puerto Rican society in cooperation with U.S. authorities. This process was completed during the populist administration of the Popular Democratic Party during the 1940s. The emergence of this new political organization and the implementation of their populist projects demanded the experience of a technocratic class trained during the years of the New Deal. Quintero and Pantojas sustain that this new technocracy would provide form and substance to the programs implemented by the newly formed populist state.[2]

Despite Quintero's and Pantojas's contributions, there are still some areas that deserve more detailed attention regarding the emergence of a strong Puerto Rican professional class and the role that it played in the PRERA during the 1930s. Certainly, one of these obscure areas that deserve more attention is the origins of the relationship between members of the Puerto Rican professional class and the American authorities on the island in the early 1930s. How did the federal government recruit these native professionals for its New Deal initiatives? How did Puerto Rican professionals perceive the progressive and modernizing agenda of New Dealers? What strategies did these professionals utilize in order to implement the New Deal agenda in Puerto Rico? Why were Puerto Rican professionals so important in the establishment of the PRERA programs on the island?

This chapter wants to focus on the seminal contribution of Puerto Rican professionals in the implementation of the PRERA programs in the island from three perspectives: First, it will expand previous analysis of the Puerto Rican professional class in the early 1930s that limits its participation to a service sector that supports the local sugar economy and was the source of the technical expertise for the populist projects of the 1940s.[3] Focusing on documentation from both the PRERA publicity offices and the local press we will able to know how the arrival of the PRERA and its progressive discourse on Puerto Rican shores was enthusiastically received by the Puerto Rican professional ranks that saw in the newly formed agency the promise of a development project with strong possibilities of transforming the material and political situations of a country battered by thirty-two years of negligent colonialism and the effects of the Depression. The arrival of the federal agency provided the members of this professional sector with opportunities for occupational mobility and growth within the ranks of the colonial administration. This section will study how local and official media contributed to create an image of the incorruptible, clean-cut Puerto Rican professional in an effort to provide credibility and legitimization to the development initiatives of the agency.

Second, the creation of a new image of the Puerto Rican professional that worked for the PRERA required an individual committed to the progressive philosophy of the agency. This section focuses on how these professionals shared the development aspirations of their U.S. counterparts in seeing the PRERA as a development initiative that would transform the harsh socio-economic conditions experienced on the island in the early 1930s. This chapter suggests that we consider that imperialism is not a unilateral projection of power. Instead, it provides a space in which the social elite of the country under imperial domination seek a common ground of understanding with the foreign power, negotiating and sharing common and contradictory political, economic, and even cultural values that strengthen their respective positions of power.

Third, as argued in the introduction of this book, historiographical studies of the 1930s in Puerto Rico considered this period as the emergence of a strong Puerto Rican nationalist discourse that questioned the presence of the U.S. authorities on the island. The violence generated between the members of the Nationalist Party, local authorities and the U.S. on the island reflected the growing questioning by Puerto Ricans about the legitimacy of the U.S. presence on the island. This section aims to study another aspect of Puerto Rican nationalism during the 1930s. As we will see, Puerto Rican nationalist discourse was utilized by Americans and Puerto Rican professionals to legitimate the presence of the PRERA in the eyes of the island's inhabitants. In an effort to provide acceptance of their programs among the island population, PRERA officials used appealing slogans for Puerto Ricans to consume products produced in "our country" as well as other similar propagandistic forms. These and other strategies that appealed to any sign of Puerto Rican patriotism are subject of study in the present work. They are directed to offer new perspectives about the flexibility of the nationalist discourse in Puerto Rico during the 1930s as well as the contradictory and complex conditions caused within the limits of peculiar political relationship between the U.S. and Puerto Rico.

The Construction of an Integral Bureaucrat

Early in his career as Administrator of the PRERA, James Bourne understood that the success for such a project depended on the presence and cooperation of a local professional bureaucracy committed to the ideals of progress and modernity offered by the PRERA's development initiatives. The success of the development project proposed by the PRERA demanded the training and the establishment of a professional sector committed to the modern and progressive discourses promoted by Roosevelt's New Deal programs. As a result, PRERA's high officials recruited qualified Puerto Rican professionals to important offices within the agency. It is not strange then that of twenty-six of the offices that constituted the PRERA, nineteen were occupied by Puerto Ricans, three of them by women. In addition, the PRERA and its publicity office, in close cooperation with local press, devoted most of their efforts to create an impeccable and convincing image of the typical Puerto Rican bureaucrat. The creation of this new image of the Puerto Rican white-collar worker was important to guarantee the success of the PRERA. For almost three decades, the federal government in Puerto Rico constituted a distant institution represented by the U.S. governor and other high-ranking officials. The implementation of the PRERA represented a change in this image about the federal institutions on the island. The presence of the federal government penetrated throughout virtually all aspects of Puerto Ricans lives. In order to provide credibility to the agency's program, it was then necessary to present an image of an honest, integral, efficient, and committed bureaucrat.

The construction of this efficient image in the Puerto Rican professional commenced within the highest ranks of the PRERA administration. This description ranged from the physical depiction of the individual and personal qualities to their professional background. In the case of William Font, sub-administrator of the agency, the publicity apparatus of the PRERA articulated the image of the ideal professional:

> "Mr. William Font, sub-administrator of this organization, is a young and competent Captain of our National Guard, whose uncommon intelligence and dynamism have contributed greatly to all the branches within this organization.

William is a 'well-born' person and at all times possesses the following enviable qualities: cold blood, prudence, and serenity in combination with a rapid understanding of all problems presented. All these have led to the brilliant success that the Captain has achieved in this difficult position."[4]

The description of Font provides a "youthful, active, and intelligent" image that the PRERA wanted to imprint in each one of its officials. The agency tried to reinforce this image with the military background of Font. The description includes a reference to his military career, referring to him most of the time as a "Captain" with "cold blood and self control," qualities that qualified him for the demands of the office in which he was appointed. These qualities stressed by the newspaper of the agency, *La Rehabilitación,* provided an image of efficiency and confidence necessary to find solutions to the serious problems that Puerto Rico faced in the early 1930s.

As mentioned, the local press contributed to the construction of the image of the local, clean-cut bureaucrat, in certain occasions with some poetic rhetoric. Experience and credibility constituted other characteristics that the PRERA wanted in its image of the Puerto Rican professional working for the agency. In an interview with Justo Pastor Rivera, Associate Administrator of the PRERA, journalist Fernando Bermejo wrote a colorful description of Rivera's qualities as public servant:

"It is important to have a dream, but the actions that make that dream a reality are even more important. He dreams and works to make Puerto Rico the same thing that other men with patriotism did for their respective countries. Flowery talk is the work of demagogic people. To dream and to make this dream real, in terms of prosperity and rescuing the country, is the labor of a true patriot. In Justo Pastor Rivera, we find a man of preparation, talent, and soul who will provide efficient help to complete the reconstruction plan for Puerto Rico, which has been placed in a triumphant march to the future by the dynamic arm and sincere heart of President Roosevelt."[5]

Pastor Rivera represented a cosmopolitan image of a man who had the opportunities to travel in other countries and who wanted to put to practice his experiences under the services of the PRERA. In addition, one of the objectives of the PRERA was to discourage the image of the Puerto Rican professional from local politics in an attempt to provide a fresh image of the public service bureaucrat. Subsequently, the PRERA skillfully created an image of trust, trying to separate Rivera from the demagogic traditional politician whose promises changed according to personal and partisan interests. For the PRERA, Rivera represented a trustful and talented bureaucrat that with his experience and "soul" would join President Roosevelt in his "sincere" effort to transform Puerto Rico.

Even low-level officials, such as Assistant Provost Marshall Juan Armstrong, demonstrated the effort of the PRERA to provide a new image to the daily operations of their institutions and offices. Armstrong's tasks consisted of providing information to the persons requesting relief aid in the main PRERA offices. It is interesting to note how the article focused on Armstrong's abilities and disposition to assist the public with kindness and patience:

> "Juan R. Armstrong, a competent and loyal employee, and at the same time a gentleman citizen, has earned the respect of his bosses and enjoys the affection of his friends and fellow workers. The equal of Mr. Bourne, Captain Font, Mr. Rivera, and Mr. Wilson, Armstrong possesses the character of those who know how to be a gentlemen, no matter to what class he belongs."[6]

The description of Armstrong contributed to the reconstruction of the traditional Puerto Rican public servant. Academic preparation and administrative proficiency were not enough in the new bureaucratic order envisioned by the PRERA. Tolerance, patience, and comprehension with the public and fellow coworkers were essential requirements in the day –to- day operations of the agency. Armstrong's qualities of kindness and patience operated in the daily contact with the people who received services from the PRERA. His "serene and energetic" approach to the demands of people desperate to receive services from the agency contributed to the paternalist image of the PRERA that subaltern segments of the Puerto Rican population created.

Puerto Rican historiography has traditionally overlooked the participation of Puerto Rican women in the professional ranks especially during the period in which the PRERA operated in Puerto Rico.[7] Nevertheless, the research conducted in this book suggests an active participation of Puerto Rican professional women within the high hierarchy of the PRERA. The establishment of the PRERA offices and its need for a professional corps able to carry out its agenda opened an opportunity for Puerto Rican women to demonstrate their potential as qualified administrators.

Rafaela Espino was among those women who were in charge of the administration in one of the most important offices of the PRERA: the Social Services division. It is important to note that among one of the PRERA priorities was the education and training of its personnel. Women were not excluded for such priority as demonstrated when Miss Espino was sent to Cleveland Western University to broaden her knowledge of social relief. The purpose of such action was justified in terms of expand:

> "With the purpose of expand her knowledge in the modern science of human relations in the social service and inspired by New Deal's spirit of commitment and responsibility, the PRERA's administration sent the dynamic Miss Rafaela Espino to take a course at Cleveland Western University."[8]

Espino illustrated the interest of the PRERA in training local professionals with the knowledge and academic approach produced in the main land. Most of the time this training was based on the "modern science of the human relations" in an effort to supplement the academic formation of Puerto Rican professionals. The training was aimed at facilitating the implementation of the person's technical knowledge and tempering it to the particular circumstances presented by the PRERA projects on the island. The technical expertise acquired in fields such as social services facilitated the insertion of Puerto Rican women to the professional ranks of the federal government development activities on the island. It also established the U.S. as the ultimate source of knowledge and reference point in the articulation of the development initiatives proposed by the PRERA.

Other Puerto Rican women reached key positions within the PRERA administrative structure, as illustrated by the case of Miss Celestina Zalduondo, Director of the Office of Welfare and Research:

> "The young, beautiful and talented 'Cele,' Director of the Bureau of Research and Aid, is the most important leader amongst the female officers within the staff of the administration. Since the implementation of the administration on August 19, 1933, Miss Zalduondo has used an excellent judgment to direct this important office. This little lady possesses superior academic preparation and personal qualities that are reflected in her brilliant record of her executive performance."[9]

Zalduondo already had a notable trajectory as a public servant. Her appointment to one of the most important offices within the PRERA and her excellent performance were evidence that she was a qualified professional with extraordinary administrative abilities of management and excellent academic preparation. Again the existence of women like Zalduondo indicates the existence of a sector within the professional working force that was academically, administratively proficient and readily employed by the PRERA. The language in which the article was written also aimed to preserve the traditional feminine values of the Puerto Rican women within a traditionally male-dominated field. The aesthetic and feminine images of a "beautiful" and "little lady" were combined with Zalduondo's professional abilities to administer a complex PRERA agency. The article tried to demonstrate that challenging governmental positions like the one held by Zalduondo did not undermine the femininity of women. Both qualities could coexist without questioning the traditional image that society held. Certainly, such differentiation made more acceptable the presence of women in Puerto Rico's institutional administration and helped them transcend the limits of the domestic life.

Moreover, the presence of Puerto Rican women in the PRERA's highest administrative ranks illustrates inroads in the perception of men about the place of professional women in the administrative offices of a federal agency. In a letter written to Zalduondo, ex-commissioner of the Puerto Rico Interior Department Guillermo Esteves, seemed to illustrate the changes in the male perception of women participation in administrative ranks:

> "Usually, the when a woman talks to the press she speaks of topics related to her feminine nature...poetry, music, painting or those things that naturally affect her delicate feelings. To hear her talk about land limitation, customs rights, and other dry problems of that sort, difficult to manage even for professional economist, it is amazing. It is comforting to know that men are not going to be on this journey alone, but that there will be Puerto Rican women who will contribute to the great goals of the PRERA."[10]

The comments of Esteves seem to embody the male view of the traditional image of Puerto Rican women: "delicate feelings" and a natural predisposition to music and poetry. The excellence of Zalduondo's performance in administrative tasks and her ability to manage "arid" topics represents in the eyes of Esteves in which the traditional subordinate role women were categorized in public service.

This study of the PRERA opens a new set of inquiries about the impact of the agency on professional Puerto Rican women. Far from being constrained to the limits of domestic life, educated Puerto Rican women occupied positions in high offices of the PRERA. Throughout their careers, these women faced numerous and challenging problems in the administration of their bureaucratic positions. These women, like their male counterparts, shared the same progressive discourse of the U.S. New Dealers who characterized the PRERA. The influence of the PRERA over the insertion of women into these important professional positions cannot be ignored. Far from be an instrument of imperial domination as maintained by some historiographic perspectives, the PRERA facilitated the insertion of Puerto Rican women into the professional sphere within the island's occupational market of the 1930s. It is also plausible to think that the professional experience acquired by those women in the PRERA paved the way to be considered during the implementation of the populist project of the Popular Democratic Party in the 1940s and 1950s. Such perspectives changed the way of thinking about fundamental and simplistic generalizations about the impact of the "imperial" role of the United States in Puerto Rico during the 1930s.

Another purpose of the PRERA was to reinvent the traditional image of the Puerto Rican professional in accordance with the modernizing projects contained in its development discourse. For this purpose, the propaganda displayed by the PRERA publicity office and local press aimed to reconstitute the image of the average public servant as one based on his or her academic credentials, experience, dedication, tolerance, and patience with dealing with general public demands. This was necessary to provide an image of an incorruptible public servant with the purpose of not "contaminating" him or her with the intrigue of local politics and making him or her appear trustworthy to subaltern segments of the population. Also, despite the number of women in the high administrative offices of the federal agency remaining low, the PRERA certainly contributed to demonstrating that women were able to satisfactorily perform delicate and complex administrative tasks. In the long term, such perceptions of Puerto Rican women helped them to transcend the traditional clerical image within the white collar working force.

Technical Expertise, Efficiency, Progress, and Modernity

The construction of an image of the honest, prepared, and integral professional envisioned by the PRERA had to be complemented also with other qualities that made a real and efficient public servant. Technical expertise, efficiency in the job performed, and a commitment to the progressive and modern endeavors of the PRERA were necessary requirements expected of every professional who wanted to work for the federal agency. Such qualities were illustrated when journalist Fernando Bermejo refered to Mr. Ernesto González, chief of the Division of Works, as the paradigm of correctness:

> "Mr. González possesses a broad and modern background in the branch of commerce. The order, regularity, and coordination of his department illustrate such preparation. It's easy to see that the employees under his orders show him respect. He has an easy manner with his employees, without any absurd dictatorial attitude."[11]

The office of public works constituted another example of the importance of technical expertise in PRERA administrators. This division provided jobs for the unemployed and performed public works for the improvement of the island's infrastructure. Technical proficiency became an indispensable requirement for the person that would occupy the leadership of that department. It is no wonder that Pedro Méndez was appointed as superintendent of buildings that belonged to the PRERA. His technical qualifications and experience made him the ideal candidate; he graduated from Syracuse University at the top of his class as an architect in 1926. When he came from the United States in 1933 to Puerto Rico, he designed numerous public buildings for the insular government. The description that one article assembled of this public servant emphasizes his qualities:

> "Méndez's important construction projects on the public buildings of the Puerto Rican government show the artistic lines of their architecture and their solid construction in all of the most important cities of our island. Méndez captured the admiration and respect of the administrators of the Department of the Interior as a result of his ingenious and architectonic vision."[12]

Méndez represented the combination of academic training and practical application sought by the PRERA development initiatives. In this particular case, such qualifications were seminal to the image of the PRERA throughout the island landscape. The construction of buildings was the most concrete image of the performance and progress of the PRERA because of its physical visibility and the service provided to the population. The application of Méndez's skill guaranteed that this visual exposure of the PRERA construction constituted a permanent testimony of the material transformation that the agency envisioned for the island; at the same time, it testified to the quality of local professionals in charge of the implementation of such projects.

Even the directors of the bureaucratic units who provided logistical support to the PRERA core divisions were expected to perform their duties with rigorously efficient and disciplinary standards. This is the case of the Divisions of Transportation and Property. Gabriel Sicardó, Chief of the Property Division Equipment and Transportation, exemplified the efficiency and coordination expected of any director of division of the PRERA:

> "The organization within the Division of Supplies, Property, and Transportation is admirable. Discipline, laboriousness, and efficiency exist in all the personnel. Here we breathe the true environment that characterizes the office of the U.S. government. We do not want to lose the opportunity to express our gratitude for our friend and fellow countryman, Mr. Sicardó, because with his admirable zeal and efficient performance, he has become part of the list of honorable *borincanos* that shoulder to shoulder, cooperate with the leaders of the PRERA in the effort of this agency to bring more prosperity to our country."[13]

"Discipline and efficiency" were the principles that local professionals adopted from the New Deal initiatives and that were embodied in the PRERA. The personal description of Sicardó illustrates the spirit of cooperation between the New Dealers in charge of the implementation of the PRERA in Puerto Rico and the local professionals. This cooperation of Puerto Rican professionals with the U.S. New Dealers was not a strange and isolated phenomenon. Most of the members of this thriving professional class shared the same discourse of progress and modernity with the U.S. New Dealers, and firmly believed in the development capacity of the PRERA to transform the material conditions of Puerto Rico. It was not strange then that the vocabulary employed by the Puerto Rican directors of the PRERA departments echoed the same enthusiasm of New Dealers such as Bourne, Tugwell, Hichock, and Johnstone. The success of the development initiatives of the

PRERA and their possibilities of transforming the economic and social conditions of Puerto Rico reflected an intent by local professionals and U.S. authorities to establish a consensus to govern the island without renouncing the colonial "rights" that the United States had established in 1898. This consensus has been constantly overlooked by Puerto Rican historiography, creating a vacuum regarding the studies of the complex institutional processes that characterized that decade.

Despite the professional and academic standards required by the PRERA administrators to perform their duties, some exceptions were made based on the merits and experience of a particular individual. The case of Pedro Arán, head of the Educational Division of the agency, demonstrated that sometimes experience was a more important element in the selection of the agency's bureaucratic personnel. Starting his career as a rural teacher, Arán occupied the office of General Director of the Rural Education Department in 1931. In 1934, he became the head of the Educational Division of the PRERA, as explained in *La Rehabilitación*. The journalist described him as the paradigm of the model teacher and public servant: "Some men that lack academic credentials, but their love for the ideals to which they have dedicated their lives mean more than academic title. Mr. Pedro Arán is one of these men."[14]

Experience, as illustrated by this quote, was regarded by PRERA officials as a relevant element in the selection of the directive personnel of the agency. Moreover, the selection of personnel without formal education credentials demonstrated that not all of the bureaucratic officials of the PRERA came from a *hacendado* class that had access to higher education, as maintained by Quintero's and Pantojas's analysis of the Puerto Rican professional. The presence of people like Arán suggests that PRERA bureaucratic opportunities were occupied by a broad class of participation that was not circumscribed to the members of a *hacendado* class eager to recuperate its power.

The efficiency and technical expertise expected from these Puerto Rican professionals in the PRERA also helped to articulate a new image of this sector *vís-a-vís* to their American counterparts. William Font, Assistant Director of the PRERA, contributed to enhancing the image of the Puerto Rican professional. He pointed out that despite insufficient resources and the lack of well-trained personnel the PRERA was able to accomplish its mission because of the capacity possessed by

Puerto Rican professionals in order to accomplish its duties. The Puerto Rican elite contributed significantly not only to reserve for themselves a share of the colonial administration, but also to support an image of self-sufficiency in the administration and the efficient implementation of the development plans to be implemented in the country. This is illustrated in Font's description of the performance of Puerto Rican social workers:

> "In the initial stages of this work, the Puerto Rican character provided proof of its admirable intuition and demonstrated the beautiful virtues of talent, comprehension, and tolerance. Despite the hard circumstances and the lack of adequate training, our social workers superseded the work of their American counterparts in terms of the weekly average of work. I extend my gratitude to all Puerto Ricans who, with a profound sense of duty and responsibility, have cooperated in an efficient way with us in the difficult task of setting the foundations of a solid and definite rehabilitation of our Puerto Rican economy."[15]

The impact of the PRERA on Puerto Rican professional ranks constitutes a watershed in the conditions of this sector within Puerto Rican society and their relations with the metropolitan state. Through the organizational values, the commitment to technical expertise and progressive approach to the traditional problems of the island Puerto Rican professionals joined U.S. New Dealers in their efforts to establish this agency as a development project. Puerto Rican professionals believed in this progressive discourse and perceived the U.S. presence on the PRERA programs not as an imperial intervention, but as a partnership that would guarantee them important positions and active participation within the agency's bureaucratic structure. In order to make the premises of this project a success, it was necessary to establish a discourse to make it acceptable to subaltern sectors of the population. The next section of this chapter explores how the Puerto Rican nationalist discourse constituted an important strategy utilized by New Dealers and local professionals to make the PRERA an attractive alternative to thousands of Puerto Ricans who had been hit hard by the Depression.

Strategies of Deployment:
The PRERA as a Nationalist Discourse

In order to establish the different projects of the PRERA and obtain its acceptance at all levels of the subaltern population, it was necessary to legitimate its presence as a messianic crusade to not only save the island from its socioeconomic crisis, but to demonstrate the capacity of Puerto Ricans to do it by themselves. The nationalist discourse that permeated all sectors of Puerto Rican society throughout the 1930s offered an alternative for portraying the PRERA as a patriotic project to save the island from the Depression and improve its social, economic, and political conditions.

To understand the importance of this discourse for the legitimization of the PRERA programs in Puerto Rico, it is necessary to provide a brief background about how this discourse has been approached by local Puerto Rican historiography. As we discussed, most of the historiographical narratives about Puerto Rico during the 1930s represented the presence of the U.S. authorities on the island as one characterized by the repression against any political dissidence, the control of the island economy by U.S. corporate capital, and the implementation of the New Deal as policies to strengthen its colonial rule in Puerto Rico. As a result, the 1930s are often described as a period in which a powerful idea of Puerto Rico as a nation emerged as the response to the difficult conditions posed by the Depression and the articulation of a strong anti-American sentiment. This section demonstrates how the nationalist discourse was explained by traditional historiography and cannot be relegated only to the condemnation of the repressive measures of the metropolitan state. American New Dealers and Puerto Rican professionals were able to merge the progressive and modern projects of the PRERA within the context of a national development project. The purpose of such a strategy made it easier for the agency's administrators to present the PRERA not as an imposition from the U.S. but as a national crusade coordinated between Americans and Puerto Ricans to bring about an articulated development program able to transform their material conditions. The appropriation of the nationalist discourse by PRERA's officials contributed to broad the traditional perspective about the idea of the nation in Puerto Rico during the 1930s in two different areas. First, as we will see, the use of the Puerto Rican national discourse by PRERA officials to legitimize development initiatives demonstrates that this concept is complex and dynamic. The continuous use of PRERA's propaganda base on nationalist rhetoric and icons demonstrates this position as well the flexibility of this discourse during the 1930s in Puerto Rico. As historian Carlos Pabón points out, "far from being a determinable and unchangeable concept, the nationalist discourse became an imaginary one whose significance has been replaced in space and time."[16] Second, drawing from the concept of the nation as a discourse that embodies multiple perspectives, the PRERA was able to establish a consensus between the metropolitan state, the native professionals, political elite, and subaltern sectors of Puerto Rican society to accept the development premises of this agency. The crux of this consensus, as we will see, lies on the efforts to represent the PRERA as a national development program in which Puerto Ricans had a strong participation in its implementation with the help of course of the metropolitan state. As a result, the PRERA was not perceived as a colonial strategy, but instead as a national crusade against poverty, ignorance, and underdevelopment.[17] The following case studies illustrate how the PRERA officials legitimated the development initiatives for the purpose previously explained.

Perhaps one of the most amazing aspects of the utilization of a Puerto Rican patriotic discourse is the fact that it was utilized not only by Puerto Ricans but by U.S. New Dealers in order to gain acceptance of PRERA programs on the island. James Bourne, administrator of the PRERA, did not hesitate to implement this strategy. Utilizing the Puerto Rican nationalist discourse, he "hybridized" the notions of love for the *patria* with the progress and modernity brought to Puerto Rico by the PRERA.[18] This command of the nationalist discourse allowed the officials of the PRERA to articulate an epic tale where the agency constituted itself as an instrument that would liberate Puerto Rico from the grasp of the Depression. As Bourne pointed out:

> "Misery demonstrates in all its extensions the countless problems that affect our country and demand immediate solution. The PRERA has been established to provide temporarily relief from the effects of all the calamities and to

provide permanent solutions. It is necessary then that we stop worrying about the problems and look for the causes of their origins. In an effort to accomplish such goals, it is necessary to asses the conditions of our present social situation in an effort to solve these problems. We are able to foment our industry, organize our agriculture, protect our products against foreign competence and rethink our political circumstances. These problems deserve our immediate attention. If we are able to focus on these goals, we will have the opportunity to enjoy a decent and a long lasting national prosperity."[19]

The declarations of Bourne regarding the mission of the PRERA on the island were quite clear. The administrator lost no opportunity to support the regime of representation that gave birth to the PRERA, describing the difficult economic conditions of Puerto Rico as "miserable and the source of all the social problems." At the same time, Bourne managed to represent the PRERA as a messianic development and national project directed to "protect our products from foreign importation" and bring "national prosperity." It is important to note how Americans such as Bourne articulated a strategy to insert the PRERA as a development project in which Puerto Rico was represented as a "nation" overlooking the colonial bonding of the island with the United States. Bourne "imagined" a colonial state that, with the development projects of the PRERA, would achieve economic self-sufficiency within the colonial relationship that existed between the two countries. Paradoxically, Bourne strengthened the colonial ties of the two countries, allowing federal government agencies like the PRERA to take an active role in the daily lives of the poverty-stricken population, showing them a more benevolent and paternalistic face of the federal government on the island. Moreover, the usage of patriotic and nationalist rhetoric helped to reflect the operation of the PRERA as a native enterprise more acceptable to the Puerto Ricans.[20] This strategy helped to dilute any attempt of Puerto Rican subaltern sectors to question in violent ways the American presence on the island and set the foundations for the colonial welfare state that would emerge in the post-World War II period.

During his tenure as administrator of the PRERA, Bourne kept hybridizing the development projects sponsored by the PRERA within a rhetoric that appealed to Puerto Rican patriotism and nationhood. On an occasion in which he was accused by local political parties of practicing favoritism in the distribution of PRERA federal funding, Bourne denied such accusations using the premises of a national reconstruction project in which he defended the actions of the PRERA, describing it as a Puerto Rican initiative to improve economic and social conditions "our work is of a national and Puerto Rican character. That is why we need the honest and disinterested cooperation of all opinion leaders of Puerto Rico."[21]

The notion of PRERA as a viable project to break the economic dependency of Puerto Rico with the United States was also shared by Puerto Rican professionals. Puerto Rican bureaucrats like Justo Rivera, Assistant Administrator like the PRERA, thought that New Deal programs as the PRERA were the base of a new national economy:

> "Among our plans is the investigation of different possibilities that our island can offer for the implementation of native industries that produce within the country the things that we actually import from other foreign countries and the United States. We think that because of our high population and the limited extension of our soil it is imperative that the development of industries that occupy the working force not be dedicated to agriculture. Rehabilitation is based on the principle that the duty of very government in the well-being of the average citizen, and if we envision to preserve our present capitalist system it will be necessary to distribute on a more equal basis our wealth. In other countries this distribution of wealth has been implemented in a violent way that does not fit within the ideology of the American institutions. The New Deal is the only way that will take us to the future within the American ideology. The New Deal will secure our right to happiness and life to all our citizens."[22]

The words of Rivera joined Bourne's rationale about inserting the premises of the PRERA policies in a Puerto Rican national project for development. At first, this could be seen as a contradiction, considering that the establishment of a federal agency on the island contradicted any strategy that defined Puerto Rico as a nation politically separate from the United States. However, the rationale to justify the PRERA as a national project was different; the PRERA was conceived not as a traditional federal relief agency but as a development project. For Rivera, Bourne, and some other sectors of the Puerto Rican intellectual, professional, and political elite, the PRERA served as a platform to break free from U.S. economic dependency. As mentioned by Rivera, the New Deal and the PRERA offered the best of both worlds: the foundations of an economic project to avoid dependency within the context of a politically stable environment.

Puerto Rican professionals intensively cooperated in the hybridization of the discourse of the PRERA and local nationalism. The notions of *patria,* prosperity, and social justice were transformed to a discourse directed at the legitimization of the PRERA development project. This hybrid of nationalism as an epic crusade to implement PRERA programs was reflected in the agency's departments and reproduced by its directive officials. The case of Ernesto González, Administrator of the Office of Works, illustrated such a process. According to González, a collective effort among Puerto Rican people needed to exist to guarantee the success of the PRERA:

> "I believe that another lesson that the PRERA taught us was to see in our hearts an altruistic feeling towards our fellow country men: more charity and comprehension of our duties and responsibilities in our work…The good citizens of a prosperous and big country where the elderly, the children, the invalids and every person that has the necessity to earn his daily bread for him and his family in an environment of dignity and justice for all."[23]

For González the presence of the PRERA on the island guaranteed a "prosperous *patria*" in which the elderly, the children, and the needy would find relief and justice. The PRERA blended itself in the image of a prosperous nation and not as an alien, imposing institution. Its programs would prompt justice and dignity in a country impacted by three decades of erratic neo-colonialism and economic chaos.

The agricultural projects sponsored by the PRERA offered another perspective of the manipulation of the nationalist discourse to the benefit of the agency. Because agriculture was the main sector of Puerto Rico's economy during the 1930s, it is not difficult to imagine why the PRERA focused enormous efforts on developing this particular area. Gabriel Correa, Director of the Agricultural Division of the PRERA, pointed out the importance of the PRERA in uniting different sectors of the country, as one nation:

> "The time is near, and we have to find a new symbol that joins us as a quiver of arrows, a symbol of the Roman unity. We have to think as Puerto Ricans and not as members of such or such a political party. If we lose time and don't take advantage of this sincere change of heart of the great nation to the north of us, all the world can judge us as criminals because we have betrayed our country and the future of our children."[24]

For Correa, the PRERA agricultural projects offered an opportunity to ignore local political conflicts and think as Puerto Ricans. The PRERA, far from being an element of separation, constituted an opportunity for national unification, sponsored paradoxically by the U.S. authorities established on the island. The penetration of the agricultural projects of the PRERA also appealed to the consumption patterns of Puerto Ricans, using again the "narrative" of the nation to create a conscience of local consumption. As argued by agronomist Antonio Defendini, the PRERA would provide the base for the development of Puerto Rico's own foodstuffs and the decline of the importation volume of this merchandise. For Defendini:

> "This island deserves a better future. The children of this island believe in patriotism but stay with their arms crossed without having any clue of what is happening in our idle country week after week. In our harbors are ships anchored with produce sent to us from the Dominican Republic. Is it not a shame to the Puerto Rican people that, having great

extensions of land without any crops, other countries have to send us the vegetables that we consume every day when the PRERA has created a division of agriculture to facilitate federal aid to 5,000 of the most needy people with vegetable seed and directions for the cultivation of these?"[25]

Defendini represented the efforts of the PRERA to provide incentives for the development of local agriculture. In order to change the consumption patterns of Puerto Ricans for certain agricultural products, Defendini criticized the lack of patriotism shown by Puerto Ricans regarding their contempt for the consumption of local products. Local consumption became a patriotic crusade, a duty that every Puerto Rican had to share in order to save the national agricultural industry. The PRERA was portrayed as the agency that would promote this national consumerism of local products, providing the necessary expertise and resources that would restore the pride of producing the food requirements that thousands of Puerto Ricans needed. The discourse employed by the PRERA in its agricultural programs illustrated how the merging of the discourses of patriotism and progress were directed to stimulate the consumption of local agricultural products by thousands of Puerto Ricans. The application of these diverse national discourses throughout the agricultural programs of the PRERA demonstrated the flexibility of those discourses as an integral part of the publicity apparatus of this New Deal agency.

Finally, the PRERA had a lasting impact on the formation of a Puerto Rican professional class receptive to the reformist plans of the Roosevelt administration. Puerto Rican professionals realized that some kind of consensus could be established between them and the U.S. government in order to improve the difficult economic conditions of Puerto Rico throughout the implementation of development initiatives. This consensus did not die with the collapse of the PRERA in 1936. This symbiotic cooperation between Puerto Rican professionals and New Dealers laid the foundation for the establishment of the Puerto Rico Reconstruction Administration (PRRA) in 1936.[26] As we will see in the next chapter, the planning and further implementation of this development plan was almost entirely a product of the initiative of a group of Puerto Ricans professionals, politicians, and intellectuals who were able to establish a consensus with the U.S. New Dealers since the early days of the PRERA. In the spring of 1934, Luis Muñoz Marín, by then Senator of the Liberal Party, Carlos Chardón, Chancellor of the University of Puerto Rico, Rafael Fernández García, Dean of the Department of Chemistry at the University of Puerto Rico, and Rafael Menéndez Ramos, an expert in agricultural business, articulated the early draft of the Chardón Plan, later to be known as the PRRA. Certainly, the PRERA constituted a watershed in the history of the Puerto Rican professional sector, allowing it to assume a key role in the implementation of the development initiatives proposed by the Roosevelt administration. Once the PRRA was established, many of its administrative positions were occupied by a substantial number of Puerto Rican officials.[27] Some of the members of these Puerto Rican elite who participated in the PRERA played an important role in some of the PRRA programs and beyond. For instance, Guillermo Esteves occupied the position of assistant administrator of the PRRA, and was responsible for the operations of the agency during its existence and its further liquidation in the early 1940s.[28] Rafaela Espino, head of the Social Service Division of the PRERA, also served in the PRRA as director of the social service unit continuing the efforts initiated by the PRERA's social division.[29] Celestina Zalduondo director of the Office of Welfare and Research of the PRERA organized diverse social services in Venezuela and directed the office of Social Welfare under the administration of the PDP in the late 1940s and 1950s.[30] Salvador Tío, former head of the PRERA's division of statistics, was appointed to direct the statistic division of the PRRA.[31] In summary, the PRERA significantly contributed to the emergence of a strong Puerto Rican professional class that made possible the implementation and acceptance of the development initiatives established, once the PRERA ceased to exist in 1936. Without a doubt, their influence transcended the collapse of the PRERA and provided the PRRA with the technocratic and bureaucratic rational for the establishment of the populist project brought by the Popular Democratic Party in the 1940s.

Notes

1. Arturo Escobar, "Power and Visibility: Development and the Invention of Management in the Third World," *Cultural Anthropology* 3 (1988):480. As Arturo Escobar explains in his analysis of the relevance of professionals: "The concept of professionalization refers to a set of techniques and disciplinary practices throughout which the generation, diffusion, and validation of knowledge are organized, managed and controlled; in other words the process by which a politics of truth is created and maintained."
2. Previous studies about the participation of this sector of Puerto Rican society have failed to provide a clear profile about the Puerto Rican professionals during the 1930s. That is why I consider this of seminal importance the inclusion of sometimes-extensive quotes to better convey the way in which these bureaucrats conceived the presence of the PRERA on the island. Ángel Quintero Rivera, *Conflictos de clase y política en Puerto Rico* (Río Piedras: Ediciones Huracán, 1986.); Ángel Quintero Rivera, *Patricios y plebeyos: burgueses, hacendados, artesanos y obreros* (Río Piedras: Ediciones Huracán, 1988); Emilio Pantojas, *Development Strategies as Ideology: Puerto Rico's Export-Led Industrialization Experience* (Boulder: Lynne Rienner Publishers, 1990).
3. I am making reference to the scholarship that has studied the social impact of the American presence in the island from 1898 to 1932. This scholarship has been mentioned and analyzed in chapter 1.
4. "Impresiones de una visita a la Rehabilitadora," *La Rehabilitación* 1 (Aug, 1934): 11, Library of Congress, Washington D.C.
5. "Justo Pastor Rivera explica los planes de la PRERA," *El Mundo*. Jan 6, 1935, 1.
6. "Algo acerca de los jefes y oficiales subalternos de la Administración de servicios de Emergencia," *La Rehabilitación* 1, (Sep, 1934.): 9, Library of Congress, Washington, D.C.
7. The lack of studies about Puerto Rico professional women during the 1930s makes it difficult to establish comparative analysis to complement the findings about this topic in the present book. However, other studies have explored the participation and transformation in the social status of Puerto Rican women in its insertion in the working force. See Félix Matos Rodríguez and Linda C. Delgado, *Puerto Rican Women's History. New Perspectives* (New York: M.E. Sharpe, 1998.); Altagracia Ortíz, *Puerto Rican Women and Work* (Philadelphia: Temple University Press, 1996); María del Carmen Baerga, *Género y trabajo: La industria de la aguja en Puerto Rico y el Caribe Hispánico* (Río Piedras: Editorial de la Universidad de Puerto Rico, 1993).
8. "La Directora del Negociado de Servicio Social en la PRERA, Srta. Rafaela Espino, se embarca hacia Estados Unidos," *La Rehabilitación* 2 (Feb,

1935.): 11, Library of Congress, Washington, D.C.
9. "Entrevista con los jefes de la administración," *La Rehabilitación* 1 (June, 1934): 5, Library of Congress, Washington, D.C.
10. "El Sr. Guillermo Esteves ex-Comisionado del Interior, dirige valiosa carta de felicitación a la Srta. Zalduondo," *La Rehabilitación* 1 (Jul, 1934): 16, Library of Congress, Washington, D.C.
11. "Los hombres de la PRERA," *La Rehabilitación* 1 (Oct, 1934.): 11, Library of Congress, Washington, D.C.
12. "El Sr. Pedro Méndez nombrado superintendente de edificios de la PRERA," *La Rehabilitación* 1 (Sep, 1935.): 18, Library of Congress, Washington, D.C.
13. "Algo acerca de los jefes y oficiales subalternos de la Administración de servicios de Emergencia," *La Rehabilitación* 1 (Sep, 1934): 9, Library of Congress, Washington, D.C.
14. "Don Pedro Arán, Director de la División Educativa de la PRERA," *La Rehabilitación* 3 (Oct, 1935): 9 Library of Congress, Washington, D.C.
15. "Discurso del Sr. William A. Font, Sub-Administrador de auxilio de emergencia, transmitido por la radio en la noche del 2 de junio de 1934," *La Rehabilitación* 1 (Jun, 1934): 11, Library of Congress, Washington, D.C.
16. Carlos Pabón, "De Albizu a Madonna: para armar y desarmar la nacionalidad," *Bordes* 1 (1995): 22-40.
17. This strategy allowed the penetration of the federal government in all aspects of Puerto Rican daily lives, strengthening over the long term the colonial regime in the island. See chapter four.
18. When I mention the term *patria*, I'm referring to the homeland. By "hybridization" I understand the study of the complex process which involves the implementation, contestation, appropriation, and negotiation of culture between two countries, in this case, between the metropolitan state and the colony. New forms of power in the metropolitan state arena as in the societies under colonial domination emerge and persist even though the foreigners withdraw. Post-colonial studies have been working with this concept for more than two decades. For more detailed information about this concept, see "Introduction," in *The Post-Colonial Studies Reader,* ed. Bill Ashcroft, Gareth Griffiths, and Helen Tiffin (London: Routledge, 1995), 183-209.
19. "Editorial," *La Rehabilitación* 1 (May, 1934): 1, Library of Congress, Washington, D.C.
20. Through the publicity office of the PRERA, local professionals articulated a publicity campaign to support the programs of the agencies directed to stimulate local economy. See figure 1.
21. "Bourne define el alcance de la representación de los partidos políticos en la isla," *La Rehabilitación* 1 (Oct, 1934): 7, Library of Congress, Washington, D.C.

22. "Justo Pastor Rivera explica los planes de la PRERA," *El Mundo*, Jan 6, 1935, 1.
23. "Los hombres de la PRERA," *La Rehabilitación* 1 (Oct, 1934.): 11, Library of Congress, Washington, D.C.
24. "La exposición agrícola de la División de Agricultura de la PRERA en Isabela," *La Rehabilitación* 2 (Jun, 1935): 8, Library of Congress, Washington, D.C.
25. "Puerto Rico, la bella isla del encanto," *La Rehabilitación* 1 (Apr, 1934): 8, Library of Congress, Washington, D.C.
26. This plan was a product of the interests of the Puerto Rican elite to improve the socio-economic conditions on the island through the implementation of development program similar to the one proposed by the PRERA. As we will see in the next chapter, the crux of this program focused on the purchase of sugar production lands and their redistribution among local producers in an effort to break with the harmful effects of the absentee corporations.
27. Interim Report on Organization of Activities of the Planning Division of the Puerto Rico Reconstruction Administration, May 28, 1936, Library of Congress, Washington, D.C. Many of the key positions of the PRRA were occupied by Puerto Rican professionals. Carlos Chardón occupied the assistant administrative position. The planing division of the PRRA was under the direction of Rafael A. Carreras one of Puerto Rico's ablest engineers. The research division was directed by Esteban Bird, the statistical unit by Salvador Tió, the engineering section by Manuel Font, the administrative section by Ramón Fortuño Sellés.
28. James C. Evans Papers, Fairbank Miles Collection, Franklin D. Roosevelt Library, Hyde Park, New York.
29. Rafaela Espino, "Trabajo social dentro de un programa de reconstrucción," *Revista de Servicio Social* 5 (1939): 23-26.
30. Nilsa Burgos, *Pioneras del trabajo social en Puerto Rico.* (Hato Rey: Publicaciones Puertorriqueñas Editores, 1997), 45-54.
31. Earl Hanson, "Interim Report on Organization and Activities of the Planning Division", May 28, 1936, Library of Congress, Washington, D.C.

CHAPTER 4

The Deployment of Development: The Implementation of the PRERA Programs and Their Impact on Puerto Rican Society

Making the New Deal Attractive to the Population

The implementation of the PRERA programs by a group of professionals committed with its promise of modernity had a significant and lasting impact on the lives of thousands of Puerto Ricans in the early 1930s. For the population of the island the presence of the PRERA in their daily lives transformed their material conditions and significantly contributed to reshape the image that they had of a distant and ineffective federal government. In order to study in more detail this process this chapter explores how the establishment and operations of the PRERA development programs penetrated the realm of the colonial subjects. The first section of this chapter concentrates on how the different programs of the PRERA penetrated the daily lives of individuals. It studies two of the most important departments of the PRERA, the Education and Agricultural divisions, as well as the penetration of the agency's programs at the municipality level. The study of the different projects sponsored by the PRERA will provide a clear picture of how the development initiatives and the modern approach to traditional "problems" on the island transformed the individual realm and material conditions of thousands of Puerto Ricans. The second part of the chapter will focus on the different ways in which people perceived, negotiated, and integrated the PRERA initiatives in their daily lives. This section will help us to understand how these processes transformed the perspectives of Puerto Ricans about the federal government on the island, allowing the emergence of a consensus that permitted the tolerance of U.S. authorities in Puerto Rico.

The PRERA Programs in the Daily Lives of Puerto Ricans

The publicity agency of the PRERA played a superb role in creating a positive image about the different initiatives implemented by the agency as exemplified in the education, agriculture, and construction programs. The Education Division constituted one of the most important development initiatives established by the PRERA. The PRERA Education Division aimed to support and complements the operations of the insular Education Department. Subsequently, it devoted its efforts to the development of two main areas: adult education and nursery programs. The purpose of the nursery schools program was to encourage the education of children, providing an acceptable environment in which they were exposed to the benefits of a quality education and medical supervision. The nurseries constituted a place where children were fed, clothed, and protected, as well as educated with the most modern and scientific educational techniques.[1] The emphasis on the nursery programs was reflected in the number of these institutions distributed throughout the island. By 1934, there were forty-nine nursery schools in existence. The programs in the nursery schools assumed control over the children as soon as they set foot in the schools. Every other day by 8:15 am, the children were brought to school by their mothers. Once there, a nurse examined the children and asked the mothers about any irregularity in the children's health. PRERA officials considered the first six years of a child's life as one of the most important periods in which an individual is formed. Consequently, good medical attention had to be provided in order to avoid any problems in the future of the child's health.[2] The nurse also inquired about the children's diet. If the diet did not meet the standards to preserve good health, a nurse would send the case to a professional nutritionist in order to prepare an adequate diet. At 9:00 am, the children went to the dining facility of the school to have a cup of milk. Once the children had their breakfast, they went to the school patio or yard. The programmed activities in the nursery reflected an attempt to expose the children to the basic skills that a "good citizen" should have. The nursery yard became a proving ground in which education tried to modify the conduct of the subjects. The description of how a child named Juanito was subject to this discipline illustrates part of this process:

> "Juanito is three years old. He learns that the slide has to be shared if every child waits for his turn. Also he learns that he has to wait until Domingo finishes using the wagon. He learns that the school property belongs to everybody and has to be shared with others. These and other multiple things contribute to his social development."[3]

The environment that surrounded these nursery schools was also important in providing a pleasant aesthetic image in which these children were placed. The nurseries were examples of efficiency and cleanliness, centers that supported the importance of teamwork and good manners. The description of school equipment indicates the integral nature in which the Education Division wanted to encompass this normalization discourse: "swings and slides and other equipment stimulated the muscular development of the children. The papers, crayons, and dolls helped stimulate the mental curiosity. The exposure to musical instruments and its coordination by the teacher formed the perspective of an orchestra. Even food was carefully planned as an effort to expose children to the taste of certain types of food not produced on the island.[4]

Another significant point was the involvement of the parents and guardians as reproducers of the material taught in class. The purpose of involving the parents was to reinforce family values and exposed them to a functional dimension within the community. Another purpose of the program was to provide the parents with the necessary skills to understand the importance of raising children in a safe environment. This included tending to their particular necessities, to providing knowledge about how family life worked, and understand the correct relationship between family and community and the way to establish this in an efficient and pleasant way. The nursery schools and their activities became the ultimate strategy to create citizens and committed colonial subjects. Parents and children had to be exposed to the benefits of a modern education committed to the progress that eventually led to the shining promise of a better future:

> "You have to see how our children thrive in our PRERA maternal schools. From early in the morning until the afternoon, our children are attended to with the most modern scientific methods that make of today's children the most beautiful of promises. The maternal schools as conceived have centers that guarantee the health and education of the children that will constitute the future of Puerto Rico. Our responsibility is to look after these children who represent the seeds of our future. These schools represent the base of the health and education of a society that in a quarter of century will be responsible for Puerto Rico occupying its position among the civilized countries of the world."[5]

The adult education programs completed the scope of the nursery program. The adult education initiatives covered the organizations of public discussions, literacy campaigns, and industrial education.[6] The subject of the discussions covered certain issues in Puerto Rican society and how they could be approached from a modern and practical perspective. These topics ranged from different ways to deal with crime, equality as the basis of education, problems of the peasantry, social and economic issues, problems that the technology had caused in modern society, eugenics, and the historical sociological problems of Puerto Ricans.[7] These discussions consisted of meetings that did not require texts, tests, or a determined number of persons. As stipulated by the PRERA, these meetings were aimed to give every person the opportunity to express their ideas with freedom and not for "propagandistic" purposes. However, the Education Division reserved for itself an absolute monopoly on the topics to be distributed in every one of the sessions.[8] In addition to the public discussions, there were other programs directed at adult instruction, such as the teaching of writing and reading to illiterate adults. The purpose of these programs was to develop the ability of adults to read printed materials, signs, and instruction, develop basic writing skills, and use printed material such as checks, postal money orders, and commercial and personal letters.[9]

Industrial education also constituted an important element in the educational initiatives proposed by the PRERA. The goal of this program was the instruction of unemployed people in manual jobs in order to provide supplemental income for the sustaining of their families. Time management was one of the objectives of the industrial education project as a way to induce workers to a healthy work ethic:

> "The division of educational activities has included in its program the organization of industrial and vocational schools for the teaching of adults. The end of these institutions is to improve the living conditions of our unemployed adults. These schools have prioritized the teaching of manual arts that will prepare the working men to use their free time to work on projects that have demand in the local market and economic benefits to them."[10]

The educational programs of the PRERA presented a laboratory in which the modernizing discourses of the PRERA were produced, transmitted, and implemented. Individuals were indoctrinated from an early age into the values represented by this new progressive order. In the nursery schools, the children were physically supervised and taught to be "good" citizens. The adult educational programs tended to complete the task initiated by the nursery schools. The adults were exposed to a broad range of educational activities that ranged from the collective discussions of topics that affected them on a daily basis to their participation in literacy and vocational education programs. Education in this context was utilized to "normalize" individuals and to make them more receptive to the modern and progressive discourse that the PRERA wished to imprint in them.

The activities of the Agricultural Division of the PRERA followed a similar agenda to the one sponsored by the Education Division, in terms of providing a modern approach to the chronic problems of Puerto Rican society. Paradoxically, the PRERA aimed to curb the most important problem that characterized the agricultural sector of Puerto Rico during three decades of U.S. domination: the cash crop economy of the island. The emergence of the sugar industry in Puerto Rico was made possible by the investment of absentee capital, which arrived as a result of the colonial integration of Puerto Rico to the United States. It is important to note how three decades after the Spanish-Cuban-American War of 1898, an agency supported by the federal government was interested in reversing an institutional policy enacted by the same government that sponsored it. Consequently, the Agricultural Division of the PRERA aimed to develop local agricultural production in an effort to curb food importation, enhance the rural economy, and provide technical support for the peasantry. Its programs centered on the promotion of agricultural expositions, the development of vegetable gardens and communal farms, and the establishment of agricultural cooperatives. The Agricultural Division, like any other PRERA development program, portrayed a modern image of the technological, administrative, and scientific progress directed to improve the material conditions of the Puerto Rican peasantry, hard-pressed by the effects of the Depression. Bienvenido Matienzo, director of the division, summarized the goals of this bureaucratic unit:

> "In addition to proportioning economic aid to our needy classes, the Agricultural Division provides the resources for the construction and cultivation of home gardens that will provide agricultural goods for home consumption. Accordingly, the Agricultural division of the PRERA, through the establishment of home and urban gardens and communal farms, has significantly contributed to the well-being of our country. The creation of these programs has encouraged our farmers to produce their own agricultural products and to defend themselves by avoiding the purchase of foodstuffs in foreign markets."[11]

The programs directed to the development of home gardens and communal farms spearheaded PRERA's agricultural initiatives. Both programs sought the development of subsistence agriculture capable of curbing the dependency of rural sectors on foreign food importation. The development of home gardens became one of the top priorities of the Agricultural Division because of its potential to end the importation of foodstuffs. For this purpose the Agricultural Division did not hesitate to use traditional methods of subsistence agriculture, such as the *conucos,* to provide a boost to its programs.[12] The home gardens were also considered a way to place Puerto Rico at the same level of other "developed" nations that produced for themselves the products that they consumed. In conclusion, the garden plan aimed at redefining agriculture at a grassroots level, instilling a sense of national pride. This pride was based on the contempt for the sugar absentee capital on which the poor peasant family depended.

The establishment of communal farms was one of the most interesting projects of the Agricultural Division. These units produced the necessary seeds for the home garden programs at cost to the peasantry. But in the long term, the communal farm programs envisioned a more complex social project. Similar to the home gardens, the communal farms tried to end the problems caused by a cash-crop economy. Accordingly, they wanted to create a medium sized agricultural sector with the purpose of diversifying Puerto Rican agriculture:

> "It is unquestionable that if the Agricultural Division succeeds in its efforts to create a class of small landowners, Puerto Rico will take the most important step for the integral and economic reconstruction of the production of food for domestic consumption, without any intermediaries that caused harm to the small farmer."[13]

Another initiative supported by the PRERA's Agricultural Division was the establishment of agricultural cooperatives throughout the island. More than mere centers of distribution of seeds and fertilizer, the cooperatives sought to develop agrarian production communities to stimulate the local market and curtail the dependence upon imported foodstuffs among the peasantry. For example, the cooperatives lent seed and fertilizer to local farmers to stimulate the production of their fields; in return, the farmers made a compromise to sell all their products to the cooperatives, which paid them 80 percent of the nominal price of the crops. The surplus generated by the peasants was then sold or bartered by cooperative officials to cooperative members, local commerce, or other cooperatives around the island. As a result, the cooperatives were not only centers of marketing of agricultural goods, but also rural social projects for the reproduction of agricultural knowledge and information:

> "The cooperative is a center of education and information for our farmers including our partners of consumption, agriculture, industrialism, and service. In other words, every cooperative has to be seen not only as a commercial and agriculture office but as a social center for the benefit of the community".[14]

Agricultural-industrial expositions were also considered a significant element in the agricultural development plan proposed by the PRERA. These expositions were designed to portray the latest developments of agricultural technology and their applicability to the development of an agricultural economy at the margin of the sugar economy. The "clean and organized" exhibitions were testimony to scientific management and material progress in the production of quality agricultural products. The exhibitions contributed to the establishment of new agricultural techniques. For instance, in the northwestern town of San Sebastián, one of the exhibits offered a workshop on how to can perishable products, how to establish flour mills, and the potential for establishing a robust livestock industry in Puerto Rico.[15] The agricultural expositions sponsored by the PRERA constituted important resources to recruit members of the rural population for its development initiatives.[16] The agricultural programs of the PRERA were aimed of breaking up the cash-crop economy and hence the dependence upon food imports caused in great part by the integration of the island by the U.S. sugar markets. The development initiatives of this important division were directed at transforming the rural society of Puerto Rico through the implementation of modern techniques of agriculture production and to redefine the island rural communities based upon the establishment of home gardens, communal farms, and agricultural cooperatives.

One of the most illustrative ways in which the PRERA demonstrated its development activities was throughout its municipal projects. These were seminal in extending the physical presence of the PRERA in the urban spaces throughout the island, placing it in intimate contact with local government institutions and the urban population. The town of Caguas offered a good example of how the PRERA established visual changes in the landscape of the municipalities. According to PRERA officials, during the 1900s through the late 1920s, Caguas was a place "where you can see the happy faces of the people enjoying excellent wages and having a pleasant life."[17] But the Depression and natural disasters drastically changed this atmosphere. The changes brought by the PRERA helped to contribute to the improvement of this town's conditions. New sanitary systems with the latest "scientific" technology were installed in the urban area and public work jobs were created as a result of the agency's presence in the town.

> "The PRERA commenced their work in the rural zone and the urban centers. Without the help of the PRERA, it would have been difficult to see improvements in the conditions of our streets. Water from sewer system has been collected in a scientific way for the benefit of the public health. And a considerable number of men were assigned to local public works earning the income for their homes. We cannot deny the *rehabilitación* (PRERA) has been something wonderful that has happened to us to normalize our lives at the most critical moment."[18]

The northwestern town of Arecibo constituted another example of how the PRERA established its presence at a municipal level. Even though the PRERA was not able to provide full assistance to the town, a partnership between the agency and the local population was coordinated to cope with different infrastructure problems. The initiatives of the PRERA were regarded as a new concern by federal authorities toward the problems of the town. The municipal government tried to reciprocate such a gesture, appealing to the town's population to get voluntary work to complement the agency's initiative:

> "Some people said that the PRERA would do everything in order to provide help to this community. But the truth is that the PRERA does not have the resources to meet the necessities of the population. The noble administration will contribute as usual to the public welfare depending of course on its resources. The people have to contribute with enthusiasm and sincere optimism to the noble cause of raising a spirit of voluntary service. This will be the time as said by a great writer in whom the spirit of the people raises again and the right of the race is reaffirmed."[19]

The PRERA was also interested in the "problems" posed by homelessness and displaced people at a city-wide level. The harsh living conditions caused by a failed economy and the coming of the Depression left considerable sectors of the population without alternatives, and many turned to begging for their subsistence. In addition to this, local authorities believed that the numbers of poor people in the urban centers of the island contradicted the modern and clean image that the PRERA and municipal authorities tried to promote. Something had to be done in order to discipline this "undesirable" population.

The case of the homeless in Coamo provides a good example of how the federal agency interacted with local municipalities to establish of municipal public policy. The town head of Coamo, Alfredo Pabón, in an attempt to deal with this problem, presented to the municipal authorities an alternative plan based on the administration of direct relief to the homeless. This plan provided to the homeless population of the town a $1.00 stipend, food, and clothes. In addition, the PRERA was also committed to organizing a non-institutional relief fund for the financial support of this program. One of the most significant aspects of this initiative was that in order to get the PRERA to offer its services to Coamo, Pabón requested that the municipal authorities enact local legislation to forbid homeless people to ask for money within the city limits. As a result of the PRERA proposal, the municipal authorities of Coamo enacted legislation following the project proposed by Mr.

Pabón. They based their rationale upon the argument that such action was a "good plan to the solution of this social problem and it is the understanding of this council that while the PRERA office is offering this relief aid there is not any reason possible that can justify begging."[20] As a result, on November 15, 1934, the local assembly approved a five-point plan based on the prohibition of begging in the town's city limits. This list included residency, physical conditions to work, time of residency in Coamo, and the names of their nearest family members. The municipal government also drafted a list of the homeless population living in the urban area of Coamo. The mayor of Coamo and local police coordinated measures to impede homeless people from other municipalities from "invading" the Coamo area. Any homeless people that failed to inscribe the municipal list would be suspended of their rights to receive relief for two weeks.[21]

Public health was another area through which the PRERA was able to penetrate the municipal realm. The mountainous town of Jayuya provided an illustrative example. The conditions of the town, described by Rafael Torres Mazorama, director of the project of social studies of the PRERA, depicted a grim scene of the health services:

> "Three months ago, Dr. Ramírez Santos, Fernós Isern, and I visited this town. We found the hospital closed and the town without any physician. The situation of Jayuya is the same as other municipalities of second and third category: In every one of these municipalities the relief aid is a caricature: there is not any medicine, the doctors never get paid, and the patients multiply as well as their illnesses."[22]

As a result of this investigation, the PRERA constructed a new hospital that included a nurse and medical personnel, a maternity ward, dental facilities, and operating rooms. The implementation of this project contributed to transforming the image of the federal government in an institution committed with the right and well being of the dispossessed people. As wished by Torres Mazzaron:

> "I hope that the federal government continues defending our rights in this way: with no selfish attitudes towards the

working class, which needs to recover its losses in health care, recuperate from a chaotic economy and enjoy the advantages that every decent government has to offer to the people."[23]

Housing projects, especially in the urban centers of the island, constituted the most visual and monumental testimonies of the development plans of the PRERA at a city level. The impact of construction upon diverse sectors of the population and the redefinition of traditional spaces effectively contributed to informing broad sectors of the population about PRERA's commitment to change their daily lives. A modern idea of how to distribute the space was imposed on the island's landscape. The physical image of this construction project constituted the most visible icon of the progress brought by the New Deal and the PRERA. As it happened in the United States, the slum clearance of the urban spaces and new forms of public housing emerged as integral components of the New Deal housing policies. In addition to providing housing to displaced sectors of the population, these programs also employed thousands of construction workers around the country. In the case of Puerto Rico, the immigration of vast segments of the rural population to the urban areas caused a great problem of urban overcrowding that was reflected in the shanty towns around the capital city of San Juan. By 1934, approximately 50,000 people lived in anti-hygienic conditions in the towns of *San Ciprián, La Zona,* and *Tras Talleres* in San Juan.[24]

One of the most important features of the construction projects of the PRERA was the emergence of housing areas for the working class. These housing projects, or *barrios obreros,* were designed to accommodate workers who imigrated from rural communities to urban centers where the economic opportunities were better. Instead of integrating this newly-arrived population into the urban landscape, the PRERA limited them to certain areas within the city limits. This was the case of the working town, or *barriada obrera de Arecibo* (working neighborhood of *Arecibo*) which included sixty families for a total of more than 300 people.[25] The *Arecibo* project aimed to provide every family with housing units that would include decent lighting, ventilation, and adequate space. But the program also envisioned the formation of functional communities based on the concept established by the Tennessee Valley Authority (TVA).[26] The administration of the *barrio* would include the services of a social worker a nurse, and a school with four classrooms. The construction of municipal halls in the towns of Arroyo and Aguas Buenas, among others, constituted symbols of the cooperation between the regional institutional powers and the federal government.[27] As stated by the representative of the PRERA in the area, Arturo de la Cruz:

> "Mr. Mayor, this building is the house of the people, as conceived by the PRERA, made possible with the help and original ideas of all the social classes. We have to admit that these projects are not the result of the work of one individual, but have been accompanied with the solidarity of all the people interested in the town's progress.[28]

The PRERA also penetrated other areas that made easier its acceptance among the island's population. By October 16, 1934, the agency assigned funds to the creation of a Fine Arts Division.[29] The activities of the Art Division supported Puerto Rican native theater, painting, drawing and music.[30] The projects involving painting and drawing classes included scholarships for talented students, restoration of Puerto Rican paint collections, and offered lectures on conservation techniques to preserve public art collections and historical buildings. The music projects funded concerts in public areas and sponsored the organization of public bands at a municipal level under the supervision of music teachers.[31] In the theater front, the PRERA funded theater programs that organized workshops for professionals and amateur actors and other people interested in this area. It also offered plays that appealed to the working class. This theater was conceived as a way to educate the working class:

> "[for the] perfection of a citizen that he will be able to defend and make respectable the rights of our nation. The working class should be allowed thorough the theater to sing their own songs, represent in the scenario their own problems in order to know their history and economy of their own country."[32]

The PRERA officials envisioned Puerto Rico as an international center for the Latin American theater with the purpose to "intensify the theater activities essential for the civilization and cultural life of every modern society."[33] The PRERA also demonstrated concerns in providing jobs to thousands of unemployed Puerto Rican women. According to the PRERA's officials, the arrival of the Depression undermined the position of the male as the only bread-winner who contributed to the subsistence of the family. As a result, diverse programs were designed to provide women with occupational space to complement their husband's meager salary. Industrial schools were established throughout the island to train women in the skills necessary to be employed in the garment industry, which would help to provide clothes to needy sectors of the population. In addition to the garment training, women were also trained on the domestic front. Courses in the fields of cooking, home maintenance, child care, and caring for sick members of the family were designed to complement the skills taught outside the domestic realm.[34]

Social activities also were organized under PRERA's auspices. In the town of Hatillo, the PRERA organized a baseball team, with the purpose of collecting money to buy cradles and chairs for babies and children. It also coordinated radio and poetry programs as the *noche hatillana* to provide an artistic space where musicians and poets of the town could display their artistic abilities. Parties and carnivals were also organized to collect funds for social service activities.[35] Care of the elderly was also an element of concern for PRERA officials. The Social Service Division of the agency also provided shelter and organized activities for elderly people throughout the island's municipalities.[36]

The PRERA programs were aimed to demonstrate to the subaltern population of the island the potential of the modern approach in order to improve their lives and establish a new regime of progress and prosperity. But through this process the PRERA also imposed a way to normalize and discipline individuals. Nursery and adult education programs aimed at exposing individuals, from their early childhood to adulthood to the gospel of a modernity that would improve their quality of life. Agriculture would provide the means to get rid of a harmful sugar cash-crop economy and destroy dependency upon imports. Municipal policies reinvented the public spaces and services of the urban centers, improving the quality of living. This regime of progress made

Puerto Ricans more dependent upon the U.S government, derailing any attempt to articulate, at least at the moment, a separate strategy to improve the socio-economic conditions of the country by themselves. Consequently, instead of weakening the colonial relationship between the two countries as a result of the effects of the Depression and the collapse of an anachronistic colonial policy, the PRERA contributed to strengthening that political situation. It is not debatable that the PRERA's publicity office did a superb job in projecting the agency's development initiatives as a crusade destined to save Puerto Rico from the harmful effects of the Depression and three decades of colonial neglect. However, in order to understand the full impact of the PRERA policies on the island it is necessary to explore how its projects represented an alternative to the abject material conditions of thousands of Puerto Ricans. Accordingly, the next section will explore the impact of the Roosevelt administration and the PRERA in the daily lives of the island's subaltern population.

Rethinking the Presence of the U.S. Government: The Subaltern Perceptions about the Development Policies of the Roosevelt Administration

The implementation of the PRERA policies would constitute a total failure without the acceptance of vast sectors of the Puerto Rican subaltern population. Starting with the election of President Franklin D. Roosevelt, thousands of Puerto Ricans started to perceive the presence of the federal government as a benevolent and paternalistic institution deeply concerned with their economic conditions. Both Roosevelt's political discourse, directed to the rescue of the "common man," and the harmful effects of the Depression contributed to change the traditional image of an unconcerned and distant metropolitan state. In addition, the implementation of programs such as the NRA and the AAA, as well as the promotion given to the New Deal as a way to solve the problems of the island, also contributed to the population "rethinking" the presence of the U.S. government in Puerto Rico. Surely, such changes of perception prepared the way for the arrival of the PRERA months later. A quick glance at a series of letters and articles written by different sectors of Puerto Rican society before the establishment of the PRERA demonstrates the multiple forms in which Puerto Ricans perceived the "new" role of the United States in their daily lives. It is important to note how for the first time in three decades, Puerto Ricans felt that they could establish a personal and direct communication with the representative of the state (in this case, Roosevelt) to solve their daily problems. No U.S. president had enjoyed such ample popularity as Roosevelt among Puerto Ricans. For example, on December 14, 1932 Manuel Palés congratulated Roosevelt for the "great triumph obtained in the November elections."[37] His confidence in Roosevelt, despite the fact that the newly elected President had not assumed leadership yet, evidences the dramatic economic circumstances experienced by the island. For Palés, Roosevelt meant the hope needed by Puerto Rico to overcome its problems:

> "In the dark hours of crisis and depression no better man could have been selected to guide the nation to a complete rehabilitation, and I feel absolutely confident that under your wise leadership not only will the states prosper, but this little island will come to a prompt and hard needed recovery."[38]

Francisco Arguloe joined Palés in his hope that the Roosevelt election would bring a new era of prosperity to Puerto Rico. Arguloe described Roosevelt as a "dynamic and great president, supreme mandatory, apostle, a general in the front of his braves troops, great economist, a truly economist among other descriptions."[39] For Arguloe, the New Deal was an epic tale able to transform not only Puerto Rico but also the rest of the world:

> "The great doctrine of the New Deal may rise like a nimbus of light and hope to establish more each day the prestige and the economic and productive power of the United States of America in Spanish America, as well as in the old continent of Europe and in the entire world. Then we shall have fulfilled a lofty patriotic duty in having contributed to the rehabilitation of our national credit and our social welfare."[40]

The optimism presented by Arguloe was also shared by people such as C.F. Figueras. Figueras, who firmly believed that the Roosevelt administration would bring substantial changes to the political relationship between the United States and Puerto Rico wrote, "our great nation will soon see the bright daylight of a new era of welfare and prosperity and do firmly that your epoch making administration will be beneficial not only to our fellow citizens but to the whole world."[41] For Figueras, Roosevelt represented a change in the colonial situation between the two countries, an opportunity to improve upon their second class-citizen status. The Roosevelt administration and its New Deal initiatives would transform the political situation of Puerto Rico by granting first-class citizenship with "full benefits" comparable to the one enjoyed by the common U.S. citizen. Others such as Adalberto González Grau and Jaime Varas, second- year high school students, joined Figueras perception of the New Deal as a chance to transform the political situation of Puerto Rico. On November 12, 1932 they wrote a letter to congratulate the newly-elected president. They also used the opportunity to demand "equal rights to all, special privileges to none, the heart of the Puerto Ricans feel for the independence and we believe that you will help us in trying to obtain it."[42] The conviction of these students makes evident how the Roosevelt administration, at least in the beginning, projected an image of concern for the people, even with the capacity to transform the colonial relationship between the U.S. and Puerto Rico. Incredibly, the down-to-earth image of an honest, integral man created around the Roosevelt persona, impressed a group of youngsters of a coastal town on Puerto Rico. These students "bought" this venerable construction of Roosevelt to a point that they felt comfortable in requesting the independence of the island from the U.S. executive, the same person who had the responsibility of enforcing the colonial relationship between both countries in years before.

One of the most interesting aspects of the construction of a benevolent metropolitan state by Puerto Ricans is the supposition that Roosevelt was able to solve their personal problems and material interests. For people like Rosa López, the president represented a chance to bring justice for her family. In January of 1933, Rosa López wrote to Roosevelt pleading for a presidential pardon to release her son, who was sentenced to nine years in prison. López, convinced of the compassionate attributions of the president, argued that she needed the support of her son in the difficult time brought on by the Depression. "Nine years in prison is such a long time she wrote, and I am so old he and I both feel that he could be a great help to me if he were here because he could work as he did before he went to the states."[43]

Others saw in the election of Roosevelt a valuable opportunity to satisfy their particular interests. A retired police officer of Bayamón, S.G. López de Azúa recognized the importance of Roosevelt as a turning point to the problems posed by the Depression to the United States and Puerto Rico.[44] In his letter, López, then owner of a private museum respectfully requested from Roosevelt an autographed photograph to place it in a "privileged spot of my personal museum to the pride of Puerto Rico, the museum and himself."[45] There were other people who saw in Roosevelt the potential of making business through his election. That is the case of Mr. José Navarro. For years, Navarro was trying to sell to the insular Department of Education a book of type-writing techniques titled the "Navarro Typewriting Book."[46] In a letter to the president, Navarro portrayed his book as a gesture "to show my gratitude to the generous American nation and to help the government in the solution of the most difficult problems in the world, I'm forwarding to you under separate cover, my book, 'The Navarro Typewriting Manual' for your examination."[47] As a way to promote the benefits of the book, Navarro appealed to the fidelity shown by Puerto Ricans to the American nation. In order to do so, he devoted one of his chapters to the study of the American flag and its significance for Puerto Ricans describing them as 99% pro-American.[48]

Others, like Cesárea Umpierre, saw in Roosevelt a way to get occupational mobility.[49] For many years Cesárea was a school principal in Caguas, a town in central-eastern part of Puerto Rico. On June 14th, 1930 she took the exam for a post office clerk with the federal Civil Service in which she received the highest score. At the time when she wrote Roosevelt, on Jan 26th, 1933 she had not received any notification about being considered in the job at the postal office, even when she knew about a vacancy in San Juan. At that point, she decided to write to the president inquiring about this job position. Cesárea's letter, as many other that thousand of Puerto Ricans wrote during that period, portraits Roosevelt as a source of justice able to solve her work problems: "It is the quality of justice and rightness which I, as all Puerto Ricans, feel that you possess and will put into the service of your country which make me write you on what some may perhaps think a very simple matter."[50]

The messianic image of Franklin D. Roosevelt was also extended to his wife Eleanor Roosevelt. It is not strange, therefore, that in March 1934, when she visited the island, many people saw in her a hope to overcome the problems brought by the Depression. The problem of the mortgage foreclosure imposed a great pressure on small and middle-sized business owners, as evidenced by the numerous documentations in relation to this situation. To Burckhart Texada, a business owner in the San Juan, Mrs. Roosevelt was his last hope in an effort to keep his home. In a letter to Mrs. Roosevelt, Texada implored that she intervene on his behalf before his creditor to avoid the execution of his home mortgage. For Texada, Mrs. Roosevelt symbolized the "providence" "with a mission to find out the human unhappiness to provide hope."[51] Another homeowner, Ramón López Bonilla, echoed Texada pleads for the intervention of Mrs. Roosevelt to save his home.[52] According to López, the mortgage executions posed a serious problem, condemning thousands to loss their property and live off of public charity. López saw in Mrs. Roosevelt his last chance, an angel of hope capable of saving him from disaster, "We hope from your human spirit do something real and help us to save our homes in order when God ask us we can says our children has a home and nobody can throw them into the street."[53]

Texada and López were not the only people who pleaded to Mrs. Roosevelt for help in an attempt to solve their personal problems. People like Josefa Micaela Ríos, who saw in Mrs. Roosevelt a great opportunity to promote her small business of garments:

> "I'm writing this letter to you as a poor widow and old woman who do not have any other shelter than the day and night. By mail, I'm sending a gift based on the garments works that I do by hand. These gifts that I made with all my heart and soul are for you and your friend Miss Lorena Hichock. Maybe if I can get your postal address I can send today more gifts to the United States."[54]

Even commercial sectors, such as the Puerto Rican Growers Association, did not hesitate to plead to Mrs. Roosevelt for help. Since the U.S. invasion of the island in 1898, the coffee industry constantly suffered from one crisis or another. Adverse tariff rates and natural disasters such as hurricanes greatly affected this industry. To make matters worse, the Agricultural Adjustment Act (AAA) made even more difficult the situation of these commercial crops by limiting its production quotas, a phenomenon which also happened to the sugar sector. For them, Mrs. Roosevelt represented the sensitivity of a newly elected administration helping the conditions of commercial sectors, not only in the continental United States but also in its territories and possessions. In a letter to Mrs. Roosevelt, the Association of Coffee Growers asked the First Lady for more access to credit, readjustments of payments to federal loans, the declaration of coffee as a basic product, forestry programs and the use of local coffee for direct relief instead of imported cocoa."[55]

Some sectors of the Puerto Rican elite also joined commercial sectors in presenting their position to the First Lady. Juanita Clavell de Cintrón, President of the women section of the Liberal Party of Ponce, clearly understood such an opportunity.[56] In a letter written to Mrs. Roosevelt, Mrs. Clavell tried to make a quick résumé of the difficult economic conditions in Puerto Rico and what they expected from the changes to be implemented by the New Deal programs in the island. More than just asking for emergency help, Mrs. Clavell reflected the interests of the middle sectors of Puerto Rican society, who wished for the establishment of long-term economic and social reforms in order to improve the conditions of the island. The interest of Mrs. Clavell in promoting a development project was related to the idea of making it an international crusade to show other countries the benefits that can be drawn from a friendly cooperation with the United States. According to Mrs. Clavell, the "present and future are one with the great American nation of which we are a part of. Let the United States show the world at large that American leadership and influence over this section of Spanish America has been inspired by other and higher aspirations than her own commercial profits or international advance."[57] Mrs. Clavell added an interesting perspective about the implementation a development plan for the island. For her, Puerto Rico became a model of cooperation with the United States that would guarantee progress and prosperity, a model which constructed the future relations between the colossus of the North and its Latin American neighbors. In some ways, this reflected the intention of the middle sectors of Puerto Rico to demonstrate to the U.S. official the possibilities to improve its relationship with Latin America by "selling" the success of any development project to be implemented on the island.

The progress brought by the PRERA and its subsequent repercussions on the colonial relationship between the United States and Puerto Rico would not have been possible without a change in how Puerto Ricans perceived the presence of the federal government. For decades, the presence of the U.S. governmental institutions represented only a distant entity to vast segments of the Puerto Rican population. The election of Roosevelt and his image as a man concerned with the problems of the common people were seminal to a more benign representation of the U.S. presence of the island. For thousands of Puerto Ricans, the Roosevelts were saviors, liberators, warriors, parents, and even commercial agents with the capacity to transform their daily lives and bring change to their terrible living conditions.

The extension of the PRERA to Puerto Rico was quickly associated with the messianic image by which Puerto Ricans perceived Roosevelt. For the subaltern sector of the island, the PRERA represented continuity with the paternalist attitude of the Roosevelt administration concerning the socio-economic problems of the island. For many people, the newly-established federal agency was considered a "machine" that would reorganize and direct the island to a future full of progress and prosperity. As an anonymous observer pointed out, the material conditions of the island were dramatically changed by the PRERA in all aspects of Puerto Rican life:

> "This hand organizes in Puerto Rico a distribution machine called the PRERA. Bread provided with Christian virtue for the needy; work, with civic dignity for the one who can render fruitful and honest work; public works, selected with intelligence to build useful things for the well-being of everybody; cultivation of the land directed with experience to multiply the production of the wealth that the country

should enjoy. The sound of that machine, from where come bread, work, wealth, and progress, is the song that the *rehabilitadora* brings to the homes and provides happiness to the spirit."[58]

The perception of the PRERA programs among subaltern sectors of the population was not limited to their impact on Puerto Rico's infrastructure. The PRERA was able to penetrate the domestic frontier of Puerto Rican society as well. The U.S. government as an alien and distant entity soon represented an alternative to the families who had been victims of the ravages of a cash-crop economy. For many Puerto Ricans unaware of the formalities of the bureaucracy, the PRERA represented a human face able to solve their most urgent problems. The image of the PRERA in the lives of these people entitled them to deal "face-to-face" with the agency without the intermission of third parties. People such as Bartolo Díaz, father of eight children, reflected on the absence of ways to communicate between the subaltern sectors of society and the welfare state:

> "We are parents of a large family without a home to provide shelter to our children. We live in a rented house and the landlord wants to evict us from the property. We want that the PRERA help us to get a job for the payment of the rent or made the necessary arrangements with the National Red Cross to get us a tent where we can live. We hope that you can understand the difficult situation in which breadwinners cannot earn enough money to feed their own children."[59]

Not everyone was happy with the PRERA's programs as illustrated by Inocencio Torres. He wrote to Lieutenant Governor Rafael Menéndez Ramos, to tell him about his suicidal tendencies as a result of the difficult economic conditions:

> For two years I have been requesting employment in the personnel division of the PRERA and have only received one answer to this letter. There is a moment in life where the father of a family experiences difficult situation as a re-

sult of the economic situation and thinks of taking his own life. Those responsible are the people that ignore the disgrace of others. The many crimes occurring in our society are the result of hunger, absence of mothers and fathers, and lack of food, clothing, and shoes. I am an educated and cultivated man in the accomplishment of my duties as a father and because I'm the one who works in this family I have to rise in anger and complain to the government that you represent.[60]

This new image of the presence of the federal government through the PRERA programs went much further than the individual cases of Díaz and Torres. In some cases, communal action created an image of the PRERA as a caretaker and provider able to solve their problems as happened in the coastal town of Santa Isabel in the southern part of the island, where parents were concerned about the closing of a scholar dining facility. For this group of parents, the PRERA lunch programs made a difference in the dietary habits and family income of this poor fishing town. The way in which this people expressed these problems to Mrs. Lang, Director of the Nutrition Division of the PRERA, connoted how this agency, as more than an alien bureaucratic structure, represented a valuable resource to overcoming the community's poverty. For these individuals Mrs. Lang did not represent another U.S. bureaucrat. When the parents appealed to Mrs. Lang as a "noble soul," with a "good heart," and "motherly feelings", they also described the human and paternalist face of the PRERA initiatives on the island:

"You do not how sorry we are about the news of the closing of the dining facility in our community and we beg you to reopen it. We also inform you of the poverty of our *barrio*. You cannot imagine the satisfaction for the parents when their children have lunch, especially when they come back from school and don't find any found at home. To your good heart and feelings as a mother we implore that you extend to this community again the benefits of a merciful and humane project. We put our faith in you and we know that you will make everything possible for our children."[61]

The perceptions that subaltern sectors of the population had about the PRERA transcended the realms of the individual, the family, and the community. According to journalist Fernando Bermejo, the PRERA was not limited to providing material relief to broad segments of the population. Instead the PRERA sought to create "self-respect as a country." In other words, the federal agency aimed to create an individual able to respect him and its government institutions:

> "The main idea of the PRERA is not only to provide better material conditions for the individual. Despite the material conditions being important, there are other moral reasons that should be more important than the problems caused by unemployment. The main idea is to preserve the self-respect for the individual and the state that governs him. The respect for self is the harmony that ultimately controls and governs the people. We are the people. We are all together the government, the church, and the school."[62]

This idea of the respectful subject, obedient to its institutions, reinforced to some extent the colonial link that tied Puerto Rico to the United States. For Bermejo, the PRERA constituted a strategy to create good citizens. Business sectors also created another image of the PRERA, as expressed by Vicente Avelino Romeu:

> "The establishment of the PRERA has helped very much. This organization has been entirely equipped by Puerto Rican merchants and is under the supervision of Puerto Ricans. All their equipment and office supplies are bought locally, thus complying with the main reason for its organization: RELIEF. The creation of the PRERA has brought a feeling of confidence to Puerto Ricans, a contrast to the feeling of uncertainty which existed a year ago. The PRERA has been, still is, and will continue fighting unemployment throughout the entire island. As a direct result, every different line of trade is getting its share. But Puerto Rico as a whole is profiting the most. New hospitals, new roads, new schools, new bridges, etc. are being built with

the exclusive use of articles produced in the U.S. but purchased in Puerto Rico and employing exclusively Puerto Ricans who are also citizens of the U.S. In a word, the entire community is being helped by the work of this Relief Administration on the island".[63]

Romeu stressed the material contributions of the federal agency in the improvement of Puerto Rico's infrastructure. Roads, schools, and hospitals paved the road for the reestablishment of Puerto Rico's self confidence. It is noteworthy how the businessman made reference to Puerto Ricans as U.S. citizens. To some extent, Romeu perceived the PRERA as a way to rescue and reaffirm the U.S. citizenship of Puerto Rico after thirty-two years of colonial domination. As a result, the PRERA not only served as a development strategy for the betterment of the island infrastructure, but as a way to rescue its colonial citizenship. The native business sector also benefited from the presence of the PRERA, selling goods and equipment to the agency and taking advantage of the improvements made to the road system of the island. Accordingly, Alberto Jiménez, businessman of the northern town of Hatillo, echoed Romeu's expressions about the positive changes brought by the PRERA to the local economy:

> "The Rehabilitation came like an angel sent by the heavens to bring peace, tranquility, and happiness to every home and started its great accomplishments, distributing food to the most needy, medical attention to the children in the schools, clothing to the poor children, work for the parents with no means to earn their subsistence, help to the local government to ease bureaucratic stress, and as a result emerged as a great project that speaks for itself. In the countryside, the agency constructs new roads and fixes the ones in poor condition, cleans up slums, and combats the mosquitoes that produce malaria that has caused so many deaths. The person who writes this letter is a representative of a North American business firm that extends its operation throughout the island. We have noted the benefits brought by the PRERA because our earnings have increased despite the rise in prices."[64]

Technical expertise in the agricultural sector was also praised by individuals throughout the island. William Jiménez refers to the agricultural technicians of the PRERA as the "khaki legion," making reference to the color of their uniforms:

> "The khaki legion, those men sent by the Agricultural Division of the PRERA to our rural areas, has provided hope to the empty soul of the peasantry, teaching them to produce not the aromatic leaves but the daily food for their children to break with the tobacco merchant or the selfish capitalist."[65]

The personnel of the "khaki legion" played a key role in the transformation of the rural landscape of the island. It is interesting that Jiménez perceived these agricultural technicians as an element that would make the peasantry transform their cash-crop economy from tobacco and sugar to producing their own food. For people like Jiménez, the PRERA signified a way to liberate Puerto Rico's rural areas from the slavery of the absentee corporate capital established on the island since the early days of the century. Initiatives such as the agricultural ones all contributed to creating a perception of the PRERA as a champion for the struggle to curb the control of absentee capital industries and to stop foodstuff importation. The agricultural exhibitions contributed to reinforcing this image. As expressed by Rafael Arjona Siaca, one of its participants, in a letter to Justo Pastor Rivera:

> "I have the pleasure of informing you that I was one of the people that visited the exposition and I was really impressed by the activities that you displayed that have helped to end the economic slavery by foreign markets. The service provided by the PRERA will be always remembered by the Puerto Rican people."[66]

The PRERA worked as a bridge towards the creation of a bureaucratic culture and the materialization of a welfare state which had been unavailable for thousands of Puerto Ricans. For the first time, the foundations and discourses of the federal government in Puerto Rico were able to penetrate more effectively the body of the subjects, making them more open to the benefits and subsequent economic dependency offered by the United States. Through this process, the PRERA was transformed from a New Deal agency into a bureaucratic unit whose responsibility was the establishment of mechanisms that made individuals more receptive to the progress brought by the New Deal. The regulative state proposed by the New Deal order portrayed an image of the government as a reliable resource that would improve material conditions. Puerto Ricans integrated these governmental initiatives and hybridized them in their cultural, economic, and political realms. This integral process was exploited by the U.S. government to establish a consensus with Puerto Ricans based upon the "benefits" brought by the existence of a regulative state and its numerous interventions in the island social realm. Despite all the changes brought by the PRERA in the local social, economic, and political arenas this agency did not last long.

Notes

1. Eugenio Astol, "Escuelas Maternales," *La Rehabilitación* 2 (Feb, 1935): 7, Library of Congress, Washington, D.C.
2. Leah Cowles, and Emma Harris, "¿Son las escuelas maternales de verdadero valor a las comunidades donde se encuentran?" *La Rehabilitación* 2 (Feb, 1935): 42, Library of Congress, Washington, D.C.
3. Leah Cowles, and Emma Harris, "¿Son las escuelas maternales de verdadero valor a las comunidades donde se encuentran?" *La Rehabilitación* 2 (Feb, 1935): 42, Library of Congress, Washington, D.C.
4. Ibid.
5. División de Publicidad de la PRERA, "La PRERA organiza en Puerto Rico la primera campaña efectiva en pro de la salud y educación de los ciudadanos del futuro," *La Rehabilitación* 3 (Aug, 1935): 15, Library of Congress, Washington, D.C.
6. Luis Muñiz, "Cómo enseñamos a los adultos analfabetos a leer y escribir," *La Rehabilitación* 2, (Feb, 1935): 20, Library of Congress, Washington, D.C.
7. Lope Bello, "El programa de las discusiones Públicas de la División Educativa," *La Rehabilitación* 2 (Feb, 1935): 20, Library of Congress, Washington, D.C.
8. "La enseñanza de adultos a través de las discusiones públicas," *La Rehabilitación* 2 (Jan, 1935): 10, Library of Congress, Washington, D.C.
9. Oscar Porrata, "The teaching of English to adult students," *La Rehabil-*

itación 2 (Feb, 1935): 23, Library of Congress, Washington, D.C.
10. Oscar Porrata, "Enseñanza industrial," *La Rehabilitación* 2 (Feb, 1935): 26, Library of Congress, Washington, D.C. The course was divided into three stages in which the students were evaluated based on their particular progress. The classes were organized into groups of thirty students that met three or two nights per week. The English courses were also designed along the same line: twenty-five or thirty students who met three or two nights per week for two hours and who were divided in three groups: beginners, intermediate, and advanced. The program aimed to develop the ability of the students to think, speak, and write in English.
11. Bienvenido Matienzo, "Intensa campaña de la División de Agricultura de la PRERA," *La Rehabilitación* 1 (Dec, 1934): 10, Library of Congress, Washington, D.C.
12. "Los home gardens y los fines que persigue la División de Agricultura de la Administración Rehabilitadora Nacional de Puerto Rico," *La Rehabilitación* 1 (Oct, 1934): 13, Library of Congress, Washington, D.C. In its efforts to eliminate food dependency, the Agricultural Division tried to establish a connection between them and the traditional *conuco* or garden plot sowed by Puerto Rican peasants: "The small garden plots and the rising of animals by our peasants was disappearing from our country side. For them their "conucos" as they called their home gardens constituted a matter of pride."
13. "Visita del Gobernador Winship a las granjas comunales de la Administración de Servicios de Emergencia," *La Rehabilitación* 1 (Sep, 1934): 19, Library of Congress, Washington, D.C.
14. Moure Carmona, "Las cooperativas agrícolas de la Administración de Auxilio de Emergencia," *La Rehabilitación* 3 (Nov, 1935): 22, Library of Congress, Washington, D.C.
15. Diego Padró, "Resultó un acto espléndido la inauguración de la exposición agrícola industrial auspiciada por la división de agricultura de la PRERA," *La Rehabilitación* 2 (Jan, 1935): 12, Library of Congress, Washington, D.C.
16. This expositions constituted a valuable opportunity used by the PRERA to expose their achievements to the general public. See figure 2.
17. "Informe sobre la situación de la ciudad de Caguas antes y después de empezar la rehabilitación en Puerto Rico," *La Rehabilitación* 2 (Apr, 1935): 8, Library of Congress, Washington, D.C.
18. Ibid.
19. "La PRERA en Arecibo," *La Rehabilitación* 2, (Apr, 1935): 24, Library of Congress, Washington, D.C.
20. R, Díaz, "La PRERA afronta el problema de la mencidad en Arecibo," *La Rehabilitación* 1 (Oct, 1934): 11, Library of Congress, Washington, D.C.
21. María Caribe, "Reparto de Ropa a los mendigos de Caguas," *La Rehabi-*

litación 2 (Mar, 1935): 24, Library of Congress, Washington, D.C. Other towns like Caguas assumed a less restrictive policy regarding the homeless, providing only immediate relief through the PRERA offices.

22. "Discurso del Sr. Torres Mazzorana en la inauguración del centro médico de Jayuya celebrada el domingo pasado," *La Rehabilitación* 2 (Apr, 1935): 11, Library of Congress, Washington, D.C.
23. Ibid.
24. R,Torres, "El grave problema de nuestros arrabales," *La Rehabilitación* 1 (Aug, 1934): 5, Library of Congress, Washington, D.C.
25. "La PRERA impulsa numerosos proyectos de hospitales y barriadas obreras," *La Rehabilitación* 1 (Sep, 1934): 6, Library of Congress, Washington, D.C.
26. For an excellent study about the concept of the TVA, see William E. Leuchtenburg, *The FDR Years: On Roosevelt and its Legacy* (New York: Columbia University Press, 1995), 159-195.
27. "La PRERA entrega el domingo pasado la alcaldía del pueblo de Arroyo," *La Rehabilitación* 2 (May, 1935): 10, Library of Congress, Washington, D.C.; "Entregando a las autoridades municipales el edificio alcaldía construido por la PRERA en Aguas Buenas" *La Rehabilitación* 3 (Sep, 1935): Library of Congress, Washington, D.C. It is important to note that the construction of *alcaldías* or, city halls, for the municipalities constituted one of the priority construction projects of the PRERA. It also constituted because of their location, one of the most visual testimonies of the developmenta projects of this agency in Puerto Rico.
28. "Entrega oficial del edificio alcaldía de Río Grande construido por la PRERA," *La Rehabilitación* 3 (Aug, 1935): 12, Library of Congress, Washington, D.C.
29. "Fine Arts Division of the Puerto Rico Emergency Relief Administration," *La Rehabilitación* 2 (Jun, 1935): 27, Library of Congress, Washington, D.C.
30. "Report of the Department of Cultural Activities and Recreation," *La Rehabilitación* 3 (Sep, 1935): 9, Library of Congress, Washington, D.C.
31. "Fine Arts Division of the Puerto Rico Emergency Relief Administration," *La Rehabilitación* 2 (Jun, 1935): 27, Library of Congress, Washington, D.C.
32. "El teatro escuela rodante para obreros," *La Rehabilitación* 3 (Jul, 1935): 17, Library of Congress, Washington, D.C.
33. Germán, P, "La obra social y cultural de la PRERA", *La Rehabilitación* 2 (Feb, 1935): 9, Library of Congress, Washington, D.C.
34. "Oportunidades creadas a la mujer por la Administración de Emergencia," *La Rehabilitación* 3 (May, 1934): 1, Library of Congress, Washington, D.C.
35. José Martínez, "La PRERA en la isla," *La Rehabilitación* 2 (Feb, 1935):

22, Library of Congress, Washington, D.C.
36. Mariano Arroyo, "Actividades del Departamento de Servicio Social," *La Rehabilitación* 2 (May, 1935): 9, Library of Congress, Washington, D.C.; "Labor social que desarrolla la PRERA en Puerto Rico," *La Rehabilitación* 2 (Apr, 1935): 11. Library of Congress, Washington, D.C.
37. Letter from Manuel Palés to Franklin D. Roosevelt, Papers of the National Committee of the Democratic Party, Dec 14, 1932, FDRL, Hyde Park, New York.
38. Ibid.
39. Letter from Francisco de Arguloe to President Roosevelt, file Fortaleza, Mar 11, 1934, General Archives of Puerto Rico, San Juan, Puerto Rico.
40. Ibid.
41. Letter from C.F. Figueras to Franklin D. Roosevelt, Papers of the National Committee of the Democratic Party, Nov 3, 1933, FDRL, Hyde Park, New York.
42. Letter from Adalberto González Brau and Jaime Varas to President Roosevelt, Papers of the National Committee of the Democratic Party, Nov 12, 1932, FDRL, Hyde Park, New York. Contreras is making reference to the policies that did not let Puerto Ricans to vote for the U.S. president.
43. Letter from Rosa López to President Roosevelt, Papers of the National Committee of the Democratic Party, Jan 25, 1933, FDRL, Hyde Park, New York.
44. Letter from López de Azua to President Roosevelt, Papers of the National Committee of the Democratic Party, Nov 9, 1932, FDRL, Hyde Park, New York.
45. Ibid.
46. Letter from José Navarro to President Roosevelt, Papers of the National Committee of the Democratic Party, Feb 13, 1933, FDRL, Hyde Park, New York.
47. Ibid.
48. Ibid.
49. Letter from Cesárea Umpierre to President Roosevelt, Papers of the National Democratic Party, Jan 26, 1933, FDRL, Hyde Park, New York.
50. Ibid.
51. Letter from A. Burckhart Texada to Mrs. Roosevelt, file Fortaleza, Mar 7, 1934, General Archives of Puerto Rico, San Juan, Puerto Rico.
52. Letter from Ramón López Bonilla to Mrs. Roosevelt, file Fortaleza, Mar 10, 1934, General Archives of Puerto Rico, San Juan, Puerto Rico.
53. Ibid.
54. Letter from Josefa Micaela Ríos to Mrs. Roosevelt, file Fortaleza, Mar 7, 1934, General Archives of Puerto Rico, San Juan, Puerto Rico.
55. Letter from coffee growers from Lares to Mrs. Roosevelt, file Fortaleza, Mar 13, 1934, General Archives of Puerto Rico, San Juan, Puerto Rico.

56. Letter from Juanita Clavell de Cintrón to Mrs. Roosevelt, file Fortaleza, Mar 8, 1934, General Archives of Puerto Rico, San Juan, Puerto Rico.
57. Ibid.
58. Observador, "La Rehabilitadora y sus efectos," *La Rehabilitación* 1, (Dec, 1934): 16, Library of Congress, Washington, D.C.
59. Letter from Bartolo Díaz to Governor Blanton, Fortaleza File, Nov 2, 1935, General Archives of Puerto Rico, San Juan, Puerto Rico.
60. Letter From Inocencio Torres to Lieutenant Governor Rafael Menéndez Ramos Winship, Fortaleza File, Jan 26, 1937, General Archives of Puerto Rico, San Juan, Puerto Rico.
61. "Peticiones de ayuda que ha recibido la Sr. Rita R. Long," *La Rehabilitación* 3 (Oct, 1935): 8, Library of Congress, Washington, D.C.
62. Fernando Bermejo, "Impresiones de la PRERA," *La Rehabilitación* 1 (Sep, 1934): 27, Library of Congress, Washington, D.C.
63. Vicente Romeu, "Puerto Rico," *La Rehabilitación* 2 (Feb, 1935): Library of Congress, Washington, D.C.
64. Alberto, Jiménez, "Opinión acerca de la Rehabilitación," *La Rehabilitación* 1 (May, 1934): 1, Library of Congress, Washington, D.C.
65. William Jiménez, "La legión kaki," *La Rehabilitación* 3 (Aug, 1935): 11, Library of Congress, Washington, D.C.
66. Rafael Arjona, "Cartas congratulatorias al Sr, Justo Pastor Rivera," *La Rehabilitación* 3 (Sep, 1935): 8, Library of Congress, Washington, D.C.

CHAPTER 5

The Limits of the PRERA as a Development Project and the Rise of a New Government Rationale

The Collapse of the PRERA as a Development Initiative

The PRERA ceased to exist as a bureaucratic dependency of the FERA in June of 1936.[1] Almost one year earlier the Puerto Rico Reconstruction Administration (PRRA) was created by President Roosevelt as an initiative to establish an alternative development project for Puerto Rico. But what were the reasons that explain this chain of events that culminated with the disappearance of the PRERA? The collapse and disappearance of the PRERA were a result of the various cumulative factors along the two-year period of its existence. U.S. inspectors of the Federal Emergency Relief Administration (FERA) evaluated the bureaucratic structure of the agency in terms of the relief provided to its population. To FERA inspectors like Vernon Northrop, the funds invested in the PRERA were insufficient to provide relief to almost two-thirds of the island's population. Northrop pointed out the possibility that the funds allocated to the PRERA were distributed in an inefficient fashion, questioning "should the relief administration attempt to do a good job for a comparatively small percentage of the total population or should it attempt to spread its funds inadequately among the whole group in need?"² Because of its centralized bureaucratic structure, Northrop argued that the PRERA increasingly depended on a large "white-collar" sector "when the majority of the people in need are in the common labor classification and receive little work relief as a result of such a distribution of funds."³ Among the recommendations of Northrop in coping with this situation were the permanent presence of a FERA official on the island and a plan to reorganize the bureaucratic structure of the agency to "provide a better basis for distributing funds to meet as much of the needs of the people for relief as possible."⁴ This concern of re-organization of the bureaucratic apparatus of the PRERA was suggested by field examiner Robert B. Watson to Harry Hopkins, director of the FERA, one year prior, concurring with Northrop that the problem to worry about was the lack of funding.⁵

Other events in the insular sphere were developing at the same time. During the years in which the PRERA was active, it received the consistent support of the Liberal Party. Since the early days of the establishment of the PRERA the Puerto Rican Liberal Party provided enthusiastic support of the implementation of the New Deal policies on the island. Crucial to this support was the presence of Luis Muñoz Marín, a young senator for the liberals in the insular legislature. Muñoz Marín, son of Luis Muñoz Rivera, former commissioner-resident in Washington and founder of the political predecessor to the Liberal Party, who was raised in the United States during his early youth.⁶ Educated in Georgetown and writing for various newspapers in the United States, Muñoz Marín was befriended during his youth prominent members of the future Roosevelt cabinet. The relationship between Muñoz Marín and James Bourne was excellent. It was not strange then that much of the personnel in the PRERA were friendly to the Liberal Party. Such a relationship was resented by the Coalition Party, which won the elections of 1932. For this political organization the fact that the Liberal minority had more access to the funds provided by the PRERA was unbearable. The result of this tension was that during the three years in which the PRERA was in operation the Coalition attacked the presence of the PRERA by concentrating its attacks on Bourne. At the same time these events occurred, Bourne was deeply concerned about the shortcomings of the PRERA, regarding its capacity to provide permanent relief to substantial portions of the Puerto Rican population. Despite his efforts to separate the PRERA from its image as relief agency, Bourne still believed that the agency had to take a definite step to establish itself as a true development reconstruction program. As stated before, Bourne envisioned the PRERA as an important step to towards making the island a self-sustaining possession without altering its political relationship with the United States. In other words, the modernizing discourse embodied in the New Deal would be the element that would draw the aspirations of Puerto Ricans to political changes with the United States. In a letter to Ernest Gruenning, Chief of the Bureau of Territories and Insular Possessions, Bourne summed up his position about any plan to be implemented for the reconstruction of Puerto Rico: "Something much more fundamental must be done to make Puerto Rico self sustaining. I believe it can be done with a reasonable investment by the federal government. This investment would be returned many times over in increased commerce with the people of the United States and decreased aid from Washington."[7]

The climax in the already deteriorated relations between local political interests and the PRERA erupted in the last months of 1934, with the attempt to establish the Rural Rehabilitation Corporation of Puerto Rico. This corporation foresaw a reconstruction program under the premises of the FERA and was implemented on the island by the PRERA; according to Bourne it presented an alternative to the Chardón Plan.[8] This was the Pandora's Box that precipitated a series of events that constituted in broad terms the final rupture between Bourne and the Coalition Party. The Coalition, well aware of the plans of Bourne to establish a plan for the reconstruction of Puerto Rico, would not tolerate another attempt by the federal official to establish another institution partially controlled by the Liberal Party. To that effect, they approved an insular Reconstruction program of its own, to challenge the one proposed by Bourne.[9] But the Coalition legislature went much further. They chose that moment to accuse Bourne and the Liberal Party of using federal funds assigned to the PRERA for the establishment of a parallel government. On March 22, 1935, the insular legislature presented a concurrent resolution "to declare James R. Bourne public enemy of the people of Puerto Rico; to inform said James R. Bourne that his presence in Puerto Rico is undesirable and to request him to leave the country as soon as possible, and for other purposes."[10] Among the accusations argued by the insular senate were the appointment of members of the opposition party (liberals) to key offices in the PRERA, the employment of persons without need paid by relief funds, the lack of professionalism demonstrated by Bourne (limited education, no executive ability, and ignorance), making of fraudulent reports, and the disruption of the commerce of the island, amongst other things.[11]

On April 4, 1934, Miguel Ángel García Méndez, speaker of the insular House of Representatives and Rafael Martínez Nadal, President of the Senate, sent a telegram to Senator Myllard Tydings requesting a full investigation of the activities of the PRERA on the island.[12] Those subsequent investigations concerning the actions of Bourne as Director resulted in the exoneration of any charges by the FERA headquarters in Washington. After this process, Bourne resigned to his post as administrator of the PRERA and took on a less-important position in the PWA.[13] In 1937, he retired from public service. Despite Bourne's departure, the idea of establishing a development initiative toward Puerto Rico did not die with the collapse of the PRERA. Puerto Rican professionals and New Dealers clearly understood that the implementation of a development project to Puerto Rico had the possibilities of improving the socio-economic conditions of the island, while at the same time preserving the existing political status between the two countries. The emergence of the Chardón Plan and the PRRA were the result of such initiatives.

The Puerto Rico Reconstruction Administration as a Continuation of the PRERA

During the spring of 1934, Liberal Senator Luis Muñoz Marín considered the possibility of challenging the local sugar interests to establish a development plan for Puerto Rico. With the help of Rafael Fernández García, the Dean of the Department of Chemistry at the University of Puerto Rico, and Carlos Chardón, Chancellor of the University of Puerto Rico, they drafted the *Plan Azucarero* (Sugar Development Plan). The early drafts of this plan proposed that the insular and federal government purchase a number of sugar refineries. These sugar refineries would be placed under the administration of local sugar producers in an effort to curb the absentee sugar capital established on the island and improve the socio-economic conditions of the population.[14] The plan was proposed in a meeting in Puerto Rico during the visit of Mrs. Roosevelt and one of the most controversial members of the brain trust, Dr. Rexford Tugwell on March 10, 1934. After the visit of Mrs. Roosevelt, Rafael Fernández García, Rafael Menéndez Ramos, and Carlos Chardón were called from Washington to articulate the premises and basis of such a reconstruction plan. This group, later called the *Comisión Puertorriqueña de Normas* (Puerto Rico Policy Commission), drafted during the months of May and June of 1934, the basis of a new development plan molded on the lines of the *Plan Azucarero* and was renamed as the *Plan Chardón* (Chardón Plan).[15]

The Puerto Rico Policy Commission proposal contained the blueprint for a more ambitious development project than that proposed by the PRERA. Following the lines of the *Plan Azucarero*, the Chardón Plan proposed determines that most of the problems faced in Puerto Rico were a result of its economic problems:

> "The economic problem of Puerto Rico, in so far as the bulk of its people are concerned, may be reduced to the simple terms of progressive landlessness, chronic unemployment, and implacable growth of the population. A policy of fundamental reconstruction should therefore contemplate the definite reduction of unemployment to a point, at least where it may be adequately dealt with by normal relief agencies, the achievement of this largely by the restoration of the land to the people that cultivate it, and the fullest development of the industrial possibilities of the island."[16]

In order to deal with these problems, the Chardón Plan followed the concept of the *Plan Azucarero* proposing broad reforms to the sugar industry production based in the purchase of sugar refineries and the redistribution of sugar production lands amongst medium- size farmers. It also proposed an extensive reorganization of the local economy in the areas of forestry, coffee, tobacco, housing programs, hydroelectric development, road construction, expansion of school facilities, slum clearance, and the establishment of Working Concentration Camps.[17]

Thus, it is not difficult to understand that the Chardón Plan constituted the logical consequence of the enlightened developmentalism proposed by most of the PRERA's programs. For instance, the agricultural projects sponsored by the PRRA found continuity with the goal of its PRERA's counterpart as we can observe in the objectives of the coffee programs sponsored by the Chardón Plan:

> "To restore production of coffee to pre-war production, that is to 40,000 or 50,000 pounds; to provide adequate hurricane insurance to the coffee plantations; restore normal credit facilities throughout debt and readjustment; to alleviate the condition of the laborers in the coffee section by substantially increasing their payrolls, providing adequate housing facilities and subsistence plots; to help in the reforestation and diminish soil erosion; to educate both farmers and laborers in intensive systems of coffee culture, in bettering their housing conditions, adapting better balancing food habits and providing for more effective medical care."[18]

The PRRA not only envisioned the development of the potential of the coffee industry and other commercial crops to contribute to the rehabilitation of Puerto Rico's economy, but it also sought to provide social services to the peasantry such as health care, good dietary habits, and decent housing. As the PRERA had previously proposed, through the implementation of its social services, the Chardón Plan aimed not only at the betterment of the economic conditions of the island but also offered the know how necessary to transform the material conditions of Puerto Ricans. The extension of such prerogatives were also found in the in the educational projects proposed by the Chardón Plan. As the PRERA did, the Chardón Plan proposed an extensive plan for the expansion of the school facilities and vocational programs: "with the development of the various agricultural programs of the Chardón Plan the education of homesteads and workers are of basic importance. This expansion plan has to be of a practical nature, along the vocational lines now operated in the island in the secondary projects."[19] Just as the PRERA, the Chardón Plan was aimed not only at the construction and expansion of the education system, but at the establishment of a vocational education system able to supply the necessities of a developing country. In some other cases Chardón adjusted his projects to the bureaucratic structure already established by the PRERA; a procedure which happened in the case of the slum clearance project initiated by the latter agency.[20] The similarities between some of the PRRA and the PRERA programs were obvious. The way in which members of the Puerto Rican intelligentsia as Carlos Chardón conceived the PRRA suggests that any initiative aimed to transform the social and economic conditions in Puerto Rico were based on the same development rational initially proposed by the PRERA.

The Chardón Plan also proposed new projects that made it different from the ones established earlier by the PRERA. However, most of these new proposals still reflected the enlightened developmentalism embodied in many of the PRERA's initiatives. As mentioned earlier, the sugar project constituted the heart of the Chardón Plan. The plan proposed the purchase of land dedicated for the cultivation of sugar from the absentee corporations. This land would be distributed among small and medium-sized sugar farmers or *colonos* for the production of sugar in government owned refineries. In order to accomplish this goal, Chardón proposed legislation for the enforcement of the Five Hundred Acres Law of 1917 that limited the usage of land by sugar refineries to 500 hundred acres.[21] This land had to be redistributed among homestead farmers for the production of subsistence crops. One of the most important aspects of the sugar plans was the establishment of cooperatives. As proposed by the PRERA earlier, the Chardón Plan sponsored the establishment of commercial cooperatives amongst the farmers who would facilitate the acquisition of credit, materials and technical assistance for the agricultural operations.[22] Chardón's intent thorough the establishment of the sugar plan aimed for the establishment of a close cooperation between the local government and the metropolitan state at the expense of the sugar corporate sector in order to articulate a rational project of development for Puerto Rico. Along this process we can perceive a strong presence of the development rational of the PRERA regarding the great necessity of establish subsistence agriculture, cooperatives, and a better use of the land to stimulate local economic growth. Chardon's sugar project faced numerous attacks by the sugar corporations and by the local political establishment in the implementation of such a program. Despite its limited success, this program and its development initiatives inspired the agricultural reform proposed by the PDP, once in power during the early 1940s.

Of all the new development initiatives proposed by the Chardón Plan, it is necessary to mention the establishment of the worker's training camps. These camps were created to supply workers for the construction of the hydroelectric plants, public buildings and roads project sponsored by the Plan. Resembling a military base, the workers lived in these camps in army-type tents equipped with quarters, kitchens, and mess halls under the command of two Army Reserve Officers. The work was scheduled for eight hours a day and the weekends were devoted to educational, civic activities, and athletics. But the purpose of these camps was not only limited to provide work to the enormous mass of unemployed Puerto Rican workers. As proposed by Chardón in the early drafts of his plan:

> "These worker's concentration camps, besides raising the efficiency and morals of the laborers, will serve also for useful educational services, teaching the workers better standards of living, using better balanced diets, birth control measures and will help to raise the measure of responsibility of the mass of workers in Puerto Rico."[23]

From the educational sections that included information concerning the betterment of the living conditions, to the importance of birth control techniques, the camps became in the ultimate center of distribution of knowledge. As occurred with the education and social projects of the PRERA, Chardón visualized the working camp as a strategy to "teach" Puerto Ricans in the ways of the modernity offered by the United States. In this aspect, Chardon's proposal maintains continuity with the PRERA's development rational in its attempt to induce and expose individuals to the "benefits" of modernity as a method to achieve progress.

Another Chardón Plan proposed a project to expand the academic programs and facilities of the University of Puerto Rico. For that purpose the PRRA assigned funds for the expansion of the university facilities, the establishment of academic relations with other universities in the United States, Europe, and Latin America, the creation of new graduate programs with special emphasis in agriculture and medicine and the establishment of an endowment fund. The PRRA envisioned the mission of the University of Puerto Rico as a "promising educational experiment in inter-American cultural intercourse."[24] The university would become a bridge between the United States and the countries of Spanish heritage:

> "With our strength in medicine and agriculture, we are gradually laying the foundation for a great institution,-unique in its kind- to serve the two Americas. Puerto Rico is becoming the center of a cultural triangle whose corners are: Spain to preserve tradition and the purity of language, as well as to maintain a point of contact with European culture; the United States, serving as an inspiration in democratic thought with its great educational centers, Columbia, Boston, Cornell Universities with a different language, with its great advances in technology and organized social efforts; and finally at the apex, Hispanic America, "the land of promise" the vast continent of immense natural wealth, little touched by human enterprise, peopled by a race of our common stocks, that speak our language, a race whom continental Americans have wholly failed to understand, due to past diplomatic blunders and to the preponderance of exclusively dollar seeking agents."[25]

Providing emphasis on the development of a prestigious university center, Chardón added to his development program an international dimension that superseded any attempt made by the PRERA development projects especially with Latin America. Denouncing the failure of the United States to understand and establish better diplomatic relations with Latin America, Chardón proposed a new approach using Puerto Rico as a model. For Chardón, the University of Puerto Rico represented "the center of a cultural triangle", a model of how a Caribbean colony was able to preserve their Spanish cultural heritage in close cooperation with the U.S. democratic traditions. The University of Puerto Rico would prove that different cultural backgrounds were able to co-exist and establish friendly cultural, technological, and social relations. Chardón tried to "sell" his university plan from different positions. For instance, he approached the problem that racial discrimination would pose for this project. His reference to Latin America as "peopled by a race of our common stocks" represented an attempt to close the gap of racial difference appealing to a common European ancestry. He also made reference to Latin America as "a land of promise" as a reminder to the U.S. government of the economic benefits that awaited them with their neighbors in the south. Chardón arguments remind us of the proposal of former Governor Theodore Roosevelt Jr., who argued that Puerto Rico was the key to establishing a new U.S. image in Latin America after half a century of imperialist expansion. Such an approach had the possibilities of offer a change of policy towards Latin America using the Chardón plan as a model of progress and modernity product of the "good-faith negotiations" between Puerto Rico (a country of Spanish heritage) and Latin America.

Notwithstanding the extensive economic and social areas that the Chardón Plan envisioned transforming, the plan experienced political opposition and economic constrains that impeded its integral implementation. Among these difficulties was a strong opposition from sugar corporations that considered the purchase of the sugar refineries and its productive lands detrimental to its economic interests. Another problem was the necessary funding to the operation of its programs. Among the alternatives considered by Chardón was the use of the revenue collected from the sugar tax imposed by the Costigan-Jones Act for the funding of the operational aspects of the plan. This alternative was discarded by the U.S. comptroller general office, which considerate the use of these revenues illegal for the finance of the PRRA projects.[26] Finally, Chardón and his supporters agreed to approve a revolving tax coming from the income of some of the PRRA's agricultural production programs. This money would be reinvested in the agency's fund to finance its operations. Finally, after a long debate the Roosevelt administration agreed to establish the agency through an executive order. As a result the PRRA was established on May 29, 1935 "to carry out in a coordinated way all reconstruction work in Puerto Rico."[27] President Roosevelt appointed Dr. Ernest Gruening as head of the newly-formed agency. Immediately thereafter, Gruenning appointed Carlos Chardón as his assistant director.

By November of 1936, after the PRRA assumed all the programs left behind by the PRERA and other federal funds were placed within the operational parameters of the agency of which 59,100 people were employed.[28] The agency began legal procedures for the expropriation of sugar corporations which exceeded the 500 acres limits established by the Foraker Act in the early 1900s. It also purchased the Lafayette sugar refinery in the southern town of Arroyo, establishing the first sugar cooperatives envisioned by the plan. Under the auspices of the PRRA, a vast plan of rural electrification was established in the island. Completed in 1942 this project built seven hydroelectric plants, increasing the power capacity of the island.[29] In the education field, twenty-two schools were constructed and turned over to the Department of Education.[30] In the University of Puerto Rico were initiated to expand their facilities. As a result, new as the school of biology, library, normal school building, domestic science building, central tower and administration, theater and armory buildings, were erected in the university campus.[31] In the area of health, the PRRA constructed twenty two urban and 103 rural medical dispensaries and funded its personnel and operation for three years.[32] One of the most important projects implemented by the PRRA was in the area of construction. Across the island the PRRA constructed recreational parks, homes for the blind, police stations, sport stadiums, weather bureau buildings and housing projects all dotted the island. Housing projects constituted another PRRA priority. Urban housing projects were constructed in the capital city of San Juan and in the towns of Caguas and Ponce. Other projects included the construction of a cement plant later transferred to the insular government, a census, and the establishment of a cooperative for coffee farmers. The PRRA even provided funding for unfinished projects started by the PRERA.[33]

Despite these important development initiatives the PRRA was plagued by administrative and financial problems that eventually precipitated its collapse. First, throughout its existence the PRRA experienced a chronic lack of funding. The original plans of self-funding established in its foundation charter proved to be insufficient to sustain the long-term operation of its programs.[34] Second, the political situation of the island also contributed to crippling the effort of this federal agency. The Coalition, fearing that the PRRA would fell under the influence of the Liberals, as happened with the PRERA, attacked the presence of the agency arguing that it constituted a parallel government that undermined their institutional powers.[35] Third, the resignation of Rafael Fernández and Carlos Chardón as the result of administrative differences with administrator Ernest Gruenning during the fall of 1936 also caused great instability within the agency's white-collar ranks. As a result, some of the Puerto Rican professionals working with Chardón and Fernández resigned, depriving the upper ranks of the agency of a strong Puerto Rican presence.[36] Fourth, the failure of the sugar plan sponsored by the PRRA led to its eventual disappearance. Within a year of its implementation, the sugar cooperative project established in the Lafayette sugar refinery presented serious problems. Among those problems were the lack of productivity of the land cultivated by the farmers, an unsteady production of sugar cane necessary for the operations of the sugar refinery, the inability of the cooperatives to meet their financial obligations and the high cost on the cultivation process. After an evaluation, PRRA officials decided to liquidate the sugar project by 1941, depriving the agency of its most important project.[37] Finally, the violence generated between members of the Nationalist Party and local authorities contributed to weaken the cooperation spirit between New Dealers and Puerto Rican professionals in the implementation of the PRRA. By February, 1936, two members of the Nationalist Party murdered the local police chief, Colonel Elisha Riggs. These two young Nationalists were arrested and murdered in the police station by members of the force. This event caused a violent response by Ernest Gruenning, Administrator of the PRRA, who demanded a public apology by Senator Luis Muñoz Marín for the assassination of Colonel Riggs. Muñoz Marín refused, arguing that he would apologize only if the American government on the island apologized first for the assassination of the young nationalists. This stalemate ended the cooperation between the two main PRRA supporters and had a negative impact on the operations of the PRRA on the island.[38]

The funding problems, the local political attacks, the administrative struggles within the agency and the lack of interest by the Congress weakened the impact of the PRRA on the island. These problems caused the termination of the PRRA programs by the fiscal year of

1939-40 when the U.S. Congress assigned the last funds to the agency. As a result, the total liquidation of the agency's financial and material assets took place on February 15, 1955.[39] For many historians the failure of the PRERA and the PRRA meant an end to the New Deal program on the island and the beginning of the populist regime that would govern the island until the late 1960s. This analysis overlooked the importance that the PRERA had in influence the scope and goals of the PRRA and the implications that this had for the emergence of a new rational of government after the 1930s.

It is undeniable also that the language, concepts, and discourses employed in the projects proposed by the PRRA reflected continuousness with the PRERA development initiatives. However, this process has not been studied in detailed by previous historiography. The scope and goals of the leadership that mustered the administrative positions of the PRERA in the early 1930s were quite different to the PRRA's in 1935. Most of the leadership of the PRERA was constituted by Americans that perceived the New Deal as a golden opportunity to revive their old progressive ideals and put them into practice in a colonial possession ravished by poverty and neglect. These ideals of progress and modernity contained in the programs of the PRERA found broad acceptance among a local elite eager to solve the terrible material conditions of Puerto Rico. These local elite started to see the colonial rule of the United States on the island from another perspective. For many of its members of elite, the image of the United States as a distant colonial presence transformed into an entity committed to the welfare of the population. The cancellation of most of the PRERA programs by 1935 did not change this perception. Thanks to the PRERA, the PRRA inherited the goal of establishing a project of colonial developmentalism implemented by an American technocracy in a collaborative consortium of the local political elite. Traditional historiography suggests that such process constituted the platform in which the Popular Democratic Party installed its populist agenda. However, such causal explanation avoids a more complex perspective that suggest a profound change in the nature of government in Puerto Rico and the way in which its power was exercised upon the population. The next section of this chapter will address this issue.

Beyond the Collapse: The Art of Governance as a Biopolitical Strategy

As discussed in the previous section, the development initiatives brought by the PRERA did not end with its collapse or the emergence of the PRRA. Traditional historiography about this subject suggests that the experiences learned as a result of the PRERA and PRRA during the 1930s constituted the main foundation of the populist project implemented by the Popular Democratic Party in the early 1940s. Certainly, the geopolitical conditions brought by World War II and a receptive political environment in Washington were more favorable in provide Puerto Rico with a long-term development initiative in the next two decades. Despite these circumstances it would be very simple to conclude that both the PRERA and the PRRA were failed development projects whose legacies were limited to providing valuable experience to the upcoming populist project. The importance of the PRERA and the PRRA did not reside only in the development experience that the PDP and its technocracy acquired from its programs. My contention is that the PRERA as the other early New Deal initiatives implemented in Puerto Rico in the early 1930s set the conditions for the emergence of a new art of governance in Puerto Rico in the early 1930s.

Traditional historiography has studied the colonial nature of the political relationship between Puerto Rico and the United States since 1898. However, they have consistently overlooked the transformation of government during the first three decades of American rule in Puerto Rico. One of the possible explanations for this is the fact that for most of the population the newly-arrived American authorities were somewhat far and remote from their normal daily lives. To make things more complicated, Washington never had a clear cut policy on how to exercise political power upon their newly- acquired possessions.[40] In order to understand this process is necessary to study the transformation of the governmental transformation in Puerto Rico during the first three decades of the twentieth century in three stages. A first stage comprehends the period of the military occupation from 1898 to 1900. The early government presence of the United States in Puerto Rico was mainly represented by the armed forces. During this period Puerto Rico was under military rule. The military government concentrated its efforts on the establishment of infrastructure in an effort of make visible the presence of the United States in it's newly- acquired possession.[41]

A second stage in the transformation of government in Puerto Rico covers the period from 1900 to 1929. The Foraker and Jones Acts enacted during the first two years of American presence on the island established the parameters in which the U.S. government would control Puerto Rico until the early 1930s. [42] The Foraker Act completed the transition from a military government to a civilian one based on republican principles. The Jones Act established American citizenship for all the inhabitants of the island. Still, American authorities in Puerto Rico were focused on administering and enforcing the governance parameters established by the Foraker and Jones Acts. Under this "governance regime", the State did not exercise its regulatory powers upon the welfare of the population. Despite the implantation of basic infrastructure across the island and an effort to establish a cultural presence, the American government as it happened in the States keeps their hands of any initiative that involves the direct intervention of the government.[43] There is no doubt that the American government extended its laissez-faire policy beyond it continental boundaries. Despite brief periods of reforms as evidenced by the Progressive Era and national emergency events as World War I, the intervention of the government in the state institutional affairs were seen as not proper and an obstacle to free enterprise and citizens rights. The colonial nature of the political relations between Puerto Rico and the United States, as well as the relationship between the federal government and the states had important similarities. This seems to support the observations of historian Gordon Lewis when he refers to the political relationship between the United States and Puerto Rico as a one characterized by an "imperialism of neglect". [44]

A third stage in the transformation of government came as a result of the Great Depression. This national emergency that emerged as a result of a new crisis significantly transformed the relations between the government and the population. From a marginal role during the first three decades of the twentieth century in a relatively short period of time, the federal government became an intrinsic part in the lives of millions of people. As we have seen in previous chapters, the New Deal and the PRERA were instrumental in this process. For many decades, historiography has focused on the New Deal as a governmental initiative that changes the political landscape of the U.S. and redefined the relationship between the State, and the contingent sectors of American society. Such an approach has obscured the possibility to consider the New Deal as an attempt to *governmentalize* the American State during the 1930s.

In the particular case of the United States the governmentalization of the State and its biopolitical approach to the populations were taking place since the early twentieth century.[45] During the Progressive Era, the Roosevelt and Wilson's administrations demonstrated different initiatives directed to regulate biological aspects of the population.[46] During the 1930s the early New Deal programs were created based on a renewed interest on the welfare of the population. Programs as the Civilian Conservation Corps, the Public Works Administration, the National Industrial Act, the Agricultural Adjustment Act, the Wagner Act and the Social Security Act were created on the basis that the government has the responsibilities of "let live" and guarantee the well-being of its citizens.

The governmentality and biopolitical rational of the New Deal programs implemented in the continental United States were extended also to Puerto Rico in the early 1930s. The colonial developmentalism represented by the PRERA programs and its focus on regulating the biological aspects of the population were responsible for the governmentalization of the American colonial rule in Puerto Rico beginning in the early 1930s. The governmental apparatus established in the island in 1898 was transformed from an institution whose main purpose was to oversee the stability of the colonial political and economic relationship with the United States to a one committed to the administration of the well-being of the population.

A quick glance to the bureaucratic departments of the PRERA will illustrate how the biopolitical dimension of the governmentalization process. The organization and mission of each one of the PRERA'a administrative units were directed to cope with the problems that posed a threat to the population and to fulfill the government's commitment to "let live". The diversity contained in the PRERA programs reflected such intent: housing assistance to the dispossessed living in shanty towns, education programs to the illiterate adults in order to integrate them into the working force, health programs to curb child mortality and tuberculosis, birth control as a measure to face the problem of population growth, the creation of public spaces, the establishment of agriculture cooperatives to improve the productivity of self-sustain crops, and social work to establish the parameters of modern society.

The governmentalization of the colonial rule on the island throughout the PRERA programs required the support and development of a new regulatory technology to oversee the services devoted to the well being of the population. It is not strange then that the programs of the PRERA were supported by an office of statistics and social work that established an effective management, quantification, classification and observation program in which the population was under constant surveillance of the progress of their programs. Metaphorically, the Puerto Rican population was an ailing body heavily punished by thirty years of colonial domination and economic deprivation.

It is also worth noting that the regime of representation proposed by the American technocracy that administered the New Deal in close cooperation with the local political elite were key in the governmentalization of the colonial rule in Puerto Rico. People like James Bourne, Director of the PRERA and Rexford Tugwell and local politicians and intellectuals such as Justo Pastor Rivera, Luis Muñoz Marín and Carlos Chardón concurred in principle that the New Deal and the PRERA were more than mere emergency relief programs. That is why in order to guarantee its successes, it was absolutely necessary to create a discursive apparatus or representation regime that made the population to understand the PRERA as a herald of progress, civilization and modernity to the population of its Caribbean possession. This regime of representation constituted the first step towards a governmentalization process. In sum, the principles of governmentality embodied in the PRERA and the biopolitical initiatives contained in them represented the only chance to cure this body of its "illness" and at the same time provide the State with the means of exercise power on the biopolitical aspects of the population.

For many decades the historiographical representation of the New Deal and the PRERA in Puerto Rico has been relegated to the depiction of an emergency agency, or a source of intrigue in local political realm. Other historiographical studies have argued that the New Deal programs significantly contributed to articulate consent among political elites and subaltern sectors of the Puerto Rican society by the end of the 1930s.[47] Such processes set the foundations to the populist reform implemented by the Popular Democratic Party starting in the 1940s. Other traditional tendencies in Puerto Rican historiography have established that that the collapse of the PRERA represented the end of the New Deal initiatives in the island. As I discussed in previous pages my contention is that far from of being a total failure the New Deal, the PRERA implemented a complex development project that governmentalized the American colonial rule in the island in the early 1930s. Such process transformed the role of the government and the way in which it exercises power throughout the regulation of the biological aspects of the population. The legacy of such transformation changed the nature of the colonial rule established in 1898 and paved the way to a new rational of government that has lasted until the present day.

Notes

1. Letter from James Bourne to Franklin D. Roosevelt, FDR official file, Appointment 400 1935-38, Apr 21, 1936, Franklin D. Roosevelt Library, Hyde Park, New York.
2. Memorandum from Harry L. Hopkins to Vernon D. Northrop, Papers of Harry Hopkins, Field Reports, Apr 23, 1935, Franklin D. Roosevelt Library, Hyde Park, New York.
3. Ibid.
4. Ibid.
5. Report from Robert B. Watson to Harry Hopkins, file 002, Feb 7-22, 1934, Papers of Harry Hopkins, Franklin D. Roosevelt Library, Hyde Park, New York.
6. Luis Muñoz Rivera founded the Federal Party at the turn of the century, seeking statehood for Puerto Rico. By the second decade of the century, this party, along with other political tendencies, merged into the Partido Unión de Puerto Rico. During the 1920s the Union Party allied with the Republicans in the Alliance Party. By the early 1930s the alliances split up. One sector allied with the Socialist Party (Coalition) and the other became on the Liberal Party discussed in this section.
7. Letter from James Bourne to Ernest Gruening, Oct 17, 1934, RG 126, National Archives, College Park, Maryland.
8. Letter from Alvaro Ortiz to President Roosevelt, RG 126, Mar 16, 1935, National Archives, College Park, Maryland; A Bill for an Act, Record

Group 69, FERA Central Files, State Series, Nov 4, 1934, National Archives, Washington, D.C. Bourne insisted on the point that the Rural Corporation was an alternative to the Chardón Plan and would have some bureaucratic and funding independence. One of the reasons that I believe that Bourne was quite emphatic on that point is to separate any potential development plan from local political manipulation and to preserve the direction of any program for himself. This kind of possessive attitude was characteristic of Bourne during the period of transition from the PRERA to the PRRA. Letter from James Bourne to Ernest Gruening, RG 126, Dec 28, 1934, National Archives, College Park, Maryland.
9. Letter from Alvaro Ortiz to President Roosevelt, RG 126, Mar 16, 1935, National Archives, College Park, Maryland.
10. Concurrent Resolution of the Senate of Puerto Rico, FERA Central files, State Series March 1933-36, RG 69, Mar 22, 1936, NA, Washington, D.C.
11. Ibid.
12. Telegram from Miguel A. García Méndez to Myllard Tydings, FERA Central Files, State Series Mar 1933-36, RG 69, Apr 4, 1935, National Archives, Washington, D.C.; Cable from Rafael Martínez Nadal to the Chairman in the Committee on Insular Affairs, FERA Central Files, State Series Mar 1933-1936, RG 69, Apr 4, 1934, National Archives, Washington, D.C.
13. Thomas Mathews, *Puerto Rican Politics and the New Deal* (Jacksonville: University of Florida Press, 1960), 248.
14. Thomas Mathews, *Puerto Rican Politics and the New Deal* (Gainesville: University of Florida Press, 1960), 157-158.
15. Teófilo Maldonado, "El Plan Chardón, su precursor, sus orígenes, sus alternativas y su triunfo," *Revista Puerto Rico Ilustrado*, (1935): 60-65, José Lázaro Library, University of Puerto Rico, Río Piedras, Puerto Rico.
16. Report of the Puerto Rico Policy Commission, Jun 14, 1934, Puerto Rican Collection, José Lázaro Library, University of Puerto Rico, Río Piedras, Puerto Rico.
17. Memorandum to Francis Shea, Sep 23, 1935, FDR Official Papers Appointment 400, Franklin D. Roosevelt Library, Hyde Park, New York.
18. Chardón Proposed Plan, Puerto Rico Corporation, RG 126, Apr 11, 1935, National Archives, College Park, Maryland, Project # 4.
19. "La PRRA crea una sección de educación vocacional", *El Mundo*, Jan 30, 1936, 1.
20. "Progresa programa de arrabales", *El Mundo*, Jan 6, 1936, 1.
21. James Dietz, *Economic History of Puerto Rico: Institutional Change and Capitalist Development* (Princeton: Princeton University Press, 1986), 89-90.
22. "El problema azucarero en la PRRA estará en manos de cooperativas de agricultores y trabajadores, dice Chardón", *El Mundo,* Jan 22, 1936, 1.

23. Chardón Proposed Plan, Puerto Rico Corporation, RG 126, Apr 11, 1935, National Archives, College Park, Maryland, Project # 14.
24. Chardón Proposed Plan, Puerto Rico Corporation, RG 126, Apr 11, 1935, National Archives, College Park, Maryland, Project # 12.
25. Ibid., 2.
26. Mathews, 197-198.
27. Press release from the U.S. Department of the Interior, May 29 1935, FDR Official Papers Appointments 400, Franklin D. Roosevelt Library, Hyde Park New York.
28. Report of George Field to the Division of Territories, RG 126, National Archives, College Park, Maryland.
29. "Thirty-sixth Annual Report of the Governor of Puerto Rico", Oct 25, 1936. University of New York, Hunter College, New York, 96.
30. Ibid.
31. Miles Fairbank, The Chardón Plan and the Puerto Rico Reconstruction Administration 1934-1954, James C. Evan Papers, Fairbank Miles Small Collection, Franklin D. Roosevelt Library, Hyde Park, New York, 71-72.
32. Ibid., 72.
33. Ibid., 74-82.
34. Mathews, 323-324.
35. "Martínez Nadal explica la actitud coalicionista", *El Mundo,* Jan 19, 1936, 1.
36. Mathews, 273-276.
37. Miles Fairbank, The Chardón Plan and the Puerto Rico Reconstruction Administration 1934-1954, James C. Evan Papers, Fairbank Miles Small Collection, Franklin D. Roosevelt Library, Hyde Park, New York, 83.
38. Mathews, 249-255.
39. Ibid, 89-100.
40. Robert L. Beisner, *Twelve Against Empire: The Antimperialists, 1898-1900* (Chicago: McGraw Hill, 1968): Christina Duffy Burnett and Burke Marshall, *Foreign in a Domestic Sense: Puerto Rico, American Expansion, and the Constitution* (Durham: Duke University Press, 2001).
41. Fernando Picó, *Cada guaraguao, galería de oficiales norteamericanos en Puerto Rico 1898-1899* (Río Piedras: Ediciones Huracán, 1898).
42. Carmen I. Rafucci de García, *El gobierno civil y la Ley Foraker* (Río Piedras, Editorial Universitaria, 1981); María Dolores Luque de Sánchez, *La ocupación norteamericana y la ley Foraker* (la opinión pública puertorriqueña) (Río Piedras: Editorial de la Universidad de Puerto Rico, 1986).
43. Aida Negrón, *Americanization in Puerto Rico and Public School System 1900-1930,* (Rio Piedras: Ediciones Huracán, 1981); Samuel Silva Gotay, *Protestantismo y política en Puerto Rico, 1898-1930* (Río Piedras: Editorial de la Universidad de Puerto Rico, 1997).
44. Gordon Lewis, Puerto Rico, *Freedom and Power in the Caribbean* (New

York: Monthly Review Press, 1963).
45. For an explanation of the concepts of governmentality and biopolitics see Michael Foucault, *Society must be Defended*, (New York: Picador, 2003); Graham Burchell, Colin Gordon and Peter Miller, *The Foucault Effect Studies in Governmentality*, (Chicago: The Univesity of Chicago Press, 1991).
46. Steven Diner, *A Very Different Age, Americans of the Progressive Era*, (New York: Hill and Wang, 1998); Arthur S. Link & Richard L. McCormick, *Progressivism* (Illinois: Arlington Heights, 1983).
47. Gabriel *Villaronga, Toward A Discourse of Consent: Mass Mobilization and Colonial Politics in Puerto Rico, 1932-1948* (Westport: Praeger, 2004).

CONCLUSION

This book has sought to expand previous studies about the presence of the PRERA in Puerto Rico during the early 1930 and has offered an alternative perspective in three comprehensive areas. First, the PRERA was not a simple welfare agency or an imperialist initiative to strength the colonial domination of the United States in Puerto Rico. The present study has demonstrated that the operations of the PRERA in Puerto Rico went well beyond a simple welfare distribution agency. From its origins the PRERA was conceived as a carefully planned developmental institution that covered virtually all aspects of Puerto Rican social and economic life. For its implementation a regime of representation was employed to promote and justify the developmental initiatives of the PRERA on the island and its subaltern population. Education, agriculture, social services, public works, training of women, and cultural activities were examples of the complexity and variety of the PRERA services in Puerto Rico. Such diversity undermines the excessive focus of traditional scholarship by limiting the activities of the PRERA to a simple welfare federal agency.

Traditional scholarly positions about the PRERA in Puerto Rico have also sustained that this federal agency disguised a new strategy of imperial domination by the Unites States as an attempt to strengthen its colonial grip on the island. Most interpretations, such as those by *Taller de Formación Política* (TFP) and Emilio Pantojas, have agreed that the PRERA and other New Deal programs were strategies of the U.S. corporate capital to intensify its colonial ambitions in Puerto Rico. As discussed by these authors, the regulative powers of the state in areas such as labor legislation and agricultural production were strategies of the metropolitan state that, with the help of capital interests, attempted to assume the control and support of different sectors of Puerto Rican society. According to this study, the early years of the New Deal and the PRERA did not constitute a conspiracy strategy to exercise imperial domination over Puerto Rico. The short existence of programs such as the AAA and the NRA and their inability to deal with the socio-economic particularities of the island make it difficult to believe that a strategy of imperial domination assumed a prominent position in their agendas. However, it is clear that U.S. authorities on the island saw the PRERA as an alternative to redefine the way in which colonial domination would be exercised in Puerto Rico. After the deterioration of the socio-economic conditions of the island and the growing threat presented by the militant actions of the Nationalist Party, the developmental initiatives of the PRERA represented a clever solution to redefine the U.S. presence in Puerto Rico. The developmental plans presented by the PRERA allowed the United States, for the first time since 1898, to present an institutional "face" in the coexistence of the insular government in the island.

By the early 1930s and with the help of the PRERA, the U.S government assumed a prominent role on the island socio-economic affairs establishing a powerful presence in the local political arena and among the population. It was not strange then that the Coalition Party complained so much about the PRERA and its administrator James Bourne. For the leaders of this political organization, the PRERA, throughout the implementation of its projects and financial resources, challenged the influence of this local political organization on their electoral base. What is more important is that the PRERA inaugurated a new era in the colonial relationship between the United States and Puerto Rico. The federal government emerged as a powerful institution that transformed Puerto Rican political culture and penetrated virtually all socio-economic sectors of the island with its regulative policies.

Second, this text has demonstrated that the impact of the PRERA in Puerto Rico and its developmentalist initiatives generated ample support among professionals sectors and subaltern sectors of society. Previous studies on the presence of the PRERA in Puerto Rico have concentrated their efforts in studying the impact of Puerto Rican technocratic and professional sectors. Traditional scholarship has sustained that the PRERA offered an opportunity to a displaced *hacendado* class, having lost their economic wealth and social status at the hands of the U.S. corporate sugar interests, desperately looking to recuperate their social preeminence in the colonial society. As sustained by scholars Emilio González, Ángel Quintero, and Francisco Scarano, the PRERA constituted a training ground for the professional and technocratic sector that helped to articulate the populist project of the Popular Democratic Party in the 1940s.

This book has proven that the impact of the PRERA on professional sectors was more complex than previously thought. True, the PRERA was seminal in the training of a professional class in the organizational techniques, administrative efficiency, and scientific knowledge that constituted the crux of the populist project of the 1940s. But this did not imply that all the members of the professional corps of the PRERA came from a *hacendado* class as suggested by previous studies. The presence of people as Pedro Arán and Rafaela Espino evidences that people from other class extraction occupied high offices in the PRERA bureaucratic structure. It is important to understand that the programs of the PDP were not only the product of an enlightened elite, but it also included considerable sectors of Puerto Ricans who were lured by the promises of progress and modernity and who transformed the harsh socio-economic conditions of a country that was battered by three decades of colonial neglect. The participation of these incipient middle class of Puerto Rican society in the PRERA programs suggested that later PDP developmental programs were not exclusively created and implemented by the heirs of the *hacendado* class generation. These studies have also failed in explore how the professional class established a close relationship with U.S. New Dealers in establishing the developmental premises of the PRERA. As chapter four illustrates, New Dealers such as James Bourne established a close relationship with Puerto Ricans such as Justo Pastor Rivera and William Font and other top Puerto Rican officials within the PRERA bureaucratic structure. Like the U.S. New Dealers, these Puerto Rican professionals believed that the modern projects and development initiatives proposed by the PRERA constituted the only feasible strategy to save Puerto Rico from its terrible socio-economic conditions. Without a doubt, this idea continued throughout the participation of this professional class in the PRRA's developmental initiatives.

Another aspect of the developmental initiatives of the PRERA that was considered in this study was its impact upon the Puerto Rican subaltern sectors. None of the studies previously conducted about the PRERA in the last four decades have devoted their research efforts to the impact of the agency's programs in the daily lives of Puerto Ricans. The study of this federal agency on Puerto Ricans allows us to appreciate how the United States was able to exercise power and redefine the colonial relationship with Puerto Rico during the early 1930s. Puerto Ricans suddenly were exposed to the policies of a developmental project supported by the U.S. government and New Deal initiatives such as: education for their children and adults, new agricultural techniques and cooperatives to sell their products, home gardens and communal farms to stimulate subsistence agriculture and the dependency on imports, social programs that identified their basic necessities, and public works for the unemployed and improvements to the island's infrastructure. All these developmental initiatives were accompanied by a strong and well-articulated nationalist and patriotic discourse that created an image of the PRERA not as an alien and distant institution, but as a national project of reconstruction. As a result, the close relationship between U.S. government officials in Puerto Rico, Puerto Rican professionals and subaltern sectors of the population created an informal consensus that accepted and integrated the regime of progress offered by the PRERA into improving the material conditions of the island. This regime of progress made Puerto Ricans more dependent upon the U.S., derailing any attempt to articulate at least at the moment, a strategy to improve the socio-economic conditions of the country by themselves. Consequently, instead of weakening the colonial relationship between the two countries, the PRERA contributed to strengthening a colonial regime that has existed until the present day, seventy years after the collapse of this New Deal agency and its developmental initiatives.

Third, the impact of the PRERA on Puerto Rican society did not end with its collapse in 1936, but continued in the developmental initiatives of the PRRA. The problems that the PRERA experienced in terms of the opposition of local politicians and bureaucratic problems caused its eventual disappearance from Puerto Rico's socio-economic scenario. However, its short existence demonstrated that the most feasible strategy to transform the existent colonial relationship between the United States and Puerto Rico was the establishment of a developmental approach to the problems experienced on the island. This situation was clearly understood by Puerto Rican politicians and intellectuals as well as New Dealers involved in the case of Puerto Rico. As a result, the Chardón Plan, later known as the PRRA, was inspired by the developmentalist spirit of the PRERA, proposing a reconstruction program for the island that aimed to transform its most critical economic and social problems.

Despite the eventual failure of the PRERA, this agency established an important precedent that influenced the political relationship between the United States and Puerto Rico for the next seventy years. This precedent established that any changes regarding the economic and social transformations of the island would depend not on crude colonial domination, but on a consensus between professional, political, and intellectual subaltern sectors of Puerto Rican society and the metropolitan state. This consensus allowed the establishment of a colonial developmentalism in the early 1930s, in which the PRERA governmentalized the colonial presence of the American State in Puerto Rico and established new principles of governance in which power was exercised by the regulation of the living standards of the population. Such process transformed the nature of the colonial government established in 1898, establishing the foundations for a new governmental rationality and a new political relationship between the United States and Puerto Rico during the second half of the twentieth century that has remained virtually intact until the present day.

The establishment of this strategy temporarily resolved the difficult social and economic problems of the island and brought stability to the colonial order established by the United States after the Spanish-Cuban-American War in 1898. Certainly, the governmentality principles brought by the PRERA constituted its most important legacy, setting the conditions for the establishment of a new political relationship between the United States and Puerto Rico during the second-half of the twentieth century.

APPENDIX

Illustrations

Figure 1. "Be a Patriot! Protect our native industry."
Example of the PRERA propaganda in an effort
to promote local agricultural production.

EXTRAORDINARIA EXPOSICION EN BARRIO OBRERO

DE LA LABOR REALIZADA EN PUERTO RICO
POR LA
ADMINISTRACION DE AUXILIO DE EMERGENCIA

INAUGURACION OFICIAL:
AGOSTO 1o., 1935

NO DEJE DE VER, ADMIRAR Y CONOCER LAS ACTIVIDADES DESPLEGADAS POR LA **PRERA** EN BENEFICIO DE NUESTRA ISLA.

UNA VASTA LABOR EN OBRAS DE INGENIERIA, AGRICULTURA, SERVICIO SOCIAL, OBRA EDUCATIVA Y VOCACIONAL.

UNA MAGNIFICA OCASION PARA ESTUDIAR LAS OPORTUNIDADES QUE TENEMOS EN PUERTO RICO PARA EL DESARROLLO DE NUEVAS INDUSTRIAS.

TODO LO QUE SU TIERRA PRODUCE.
TODO LO QUE SU TIERRA LE BRINDA.
TODO PARA PUERTO RICO Y POR PUERTO RICO.

VEALO!   ADMIRELO!   APRENDA!

Figure 2. "Extraordinary Exposition in Barrio Obrero." Announcement of one of the PRERA's expositions.

BIBLIOGRAPHY

Government Archives

Bureau of Insular Affairs, RG 350, National Archives, Washington DC
FDR Official Papers Appointments, FDR Library, Hyde Park, New York
FERA Central Files, RG 69, National Archives, Washington DC
Fortaleza File, Puerto Rico General Archives, San Juan, Puerto Rico
Papers of Harry Hopkins, FDR Library, Hyde Park, New York
PRERA, First Annual Report, Library of Congress, Washington DC
Records of the Office of Territories, RG 126, National Archives, Washington DC

Library Collections

Governor's Annual Report, University of New York, Hunter College, Puerto Rican Collection
La Rehabilitación, Library of Congress, Washington DC

Contemporary Periodicals

El Mundo, July 10, 1933
El Mundo, July 20, 1933
El Mundo, October 29, 1933
El Mundo, November 29, 1933
El Mundo, December 4, 1933
El Mundo, December 5, 1933
El Mundo, January 6, 1935
El Mundo, January 6, 1936
El Mundo, January 19, 1936
El Mundo, January, 22, 1936
El Mundo, January 30, 1936

Secondary Sources

Ashcroft, Bill, Gareth Griffiths, and Helen Tiffin. *The Post-Colonial Studies Reader.* London: Routledge, 1995.

Baerga, María del Carmen. *Género y trabajo: la industria de la aguja en Puerto Rico y el Caribe Hispánico.* Río Piedras: Editorial de la Universidad de Puerto Rico, 1993.

Beisner, Robert. *Twelve Against Empire: The Anti-Imperialists 1898-1900.* Chicago: Imprint Publications, 2001.

Bernstein, Barton. *Towards a New Past: Dissenting Essays in American History.* New York: Pantheon Books, 1968.

Biles, Roger. *The South and the New Deal.* Lexington: University of Kentucky Press, 2006.

Bourne, James and Dorothy Bourne. *Thirty Years of Change in Puerto Rico.* New York: Frederick A. Praeger Publishers, 1966.

Brinkley, Alan. *The End of the Reform: New Deal Liberalism in Recession and War.* New York: Alfred A. Knopf, 1995.

Burchell, Graham, Colin Gordon, and Peter Miller. *The Foucault Effect: Studies in Governmentality.* Chicago: University of Chicago Press, 1991.

Burgos, Nilsa M. *Pioneras de la profesión de trabajo social en Puerto Rico.* Hato Rey: Publicaciones Puertorriqueñas, 1997.

Chafe, William. *The Achievement of American Liberalism: The New Deal and Its Legacies.* New York: Columbia University Press, 2003.

Clark, Victor S. *Porto Rico and Its Problems.* Washington DC: The Brookings Institution, 1930.

Cohen, Lizabeth. *Making a New Deal: Industrial Workers in Chicago, 1919-1939.* New York: Cambridge University Press, 1990.

Collins, Robert. "Positive Responses to the New Deal: The Roots of the Committee for Economic Development, 1933-42." *Business History Review* (Autumn 1978): 368-390.

Dietz, James. *Economic History of Puerto Rico: Institutional Change and Capitalist Development.* Princeton: Princeton University Press, 1986.

Diffie, Bailey, and Justine Diffie. *Porto Rico: A Broken Pledge.* New York: The Vanguard Press, 1931.

Diner, Steven. *A Very Different Age: Americans of the Progressive Era.*

New York: Hill and Wang, 1998.

Dolores Luque, María. *La ocupación norteamericana y la ley Foraker*. Río Piedras: Editorial de la Universidad de Puerto Rico, 1986.

Dreyfus, Herbert L., and Rabinow, Paul. *Beyond Structuralism and Hermeneutics*. Chicago: The University of Chicago Press, 1982.

Duffy, Burnett Christina, and Marshall Burke. *Foreign in a Domestic Sense: Puerto Rico, American Expansion, and the Constitution*. Durham: Duke University Press, 2001.

Escobar, Arturo. "Power and Visibility: Development and the Invention of Management in the Third World." *Cultural Anthropology* 3 (1988): 658-682.

_____. *Encountering Development: Tthe Making and Unmaking of the Third World*. Princeton: Princeton University Press, 1995.

Ferguson, James. *The Antipolitics Machine: Development, Depoliticization, and Bureaucratic Power in Lesotho*. Minneapolis: University of Minnesota Press, 1994.

Ferrao, Luis A. *Pedro Albizu Campos y el nacionalismo puertorriqueño*. Río Piedras: Editorial Edil, 1990.

Foucault, Michel. *Historia de la sexualidad la voluntad de saber*. XXI, Vol. 1. México D.F.: Siglo 1977.

_____. *Defender la sociedad*. México D.F.: Fondo de Cultura Económica, 2002.

Fraser, Steve, and Gary Gerstle. *The Rise and Fall of the New Deal Order*. Princeton: Princeton University Press, 1989.

Galambos, Louis. "Technology, Political Economy, and Professionalization: Central Themes of the Organizational Synthesis." *Business History Review* 57 (Winter 1983): 471-491.

García, Gervasio Luis, and Ángel Quintero Rivera. *Desafío y solidaridad: breve historia sobre el movimiento obrero en Puerto Rico*. Río Piedras: Ediciones Huracán, 1986.

García Pantojas, Emilio. "Estrategias de desarrollo y contradicciones ideológicas en Puerto Rico: 1940-1978." *Revista de Ciencias Sociales* 21 (Mar-Jun 1979): 73- 117.

_____. "Puerto Rican Populism Revisited: The PPD during the 1940s." *Journal of Latin American Studies* 21 (1989): 521-557.

_____. *Development Strategies as Ideology*. Boulder: Lynne Rienner Publishers, 1990.

Geertz, Clifford. *The Interpretation of Cultures*. United States: Basic Books, 1973.

González, Emilio. "La lucha de clases y la política en el Puerto Rico de la década del 40' El Ascenso del PPD." *Revista de Ciencias Sociales* 22 (Mar-Jun 1980): 35-67.

Guha, Ranajit, and Gayatri Chakravorty Spivak. *Selected Subaltern Studies*. New York: Oxford University Press, 1988.

_____. *Dominance without Hegemony*. Cambridge: Harvard University Press, 1997.

Hawley, Ellis. "The Discovery and Study of the Corporate Liberalism." *Business History Review* 52 (Autumn 1978): 308-320.

Hobsbawn, Eric. *The Invention of Tradition*. New York: Cambridge University Press, 1983.

Hoftstader, Richard. *The Age of Reform*. New York: Vintage Books, 1955.

Hunt, Lynn. *The New Cultural History*. Berkeley: University of California Press, 1989.

Joseph, Gilbert, Catherine C. Legrand, and Ricardo Salvatore, eds. *Close Encounters with Empire: Writing the Cultural History of U.S.-Latin American Relations*. Durham: Duke University Press, 1998.

Leuchtenburg, William. *Franklin D. Roosevelt and the New Deal*. New York: Harper and Row, 1963.

_____. *The FDR Years: On Roosevelt and His Legacy*. New York: Columbia University Press, 1995.

Lewis, Gordon. *Freedom and Power in the Caribbean*. New York: Monthly Review Press, 1963.

Link, Arthur S., and Richard L. McCormick. *Progressivism*. Illinois: Arlington Heights, 1983.

Luque de Sánchez, María Dolores. *La ocupación norteamericana y la ley Foraker*. Río Piedras: Editorial de la Universidad de Puerto Rico, 1986.

Maher, Neil. *Nature's New Deal: The Civilian Conservation Corps and the Roots of the American Environmental Movement*. New York: Oxford University Press, 2008.

Mathews, Thomas. *Puerto Rican Politics and the New Deal*. Gainesville: University of Florida Press, 1960.

Matos Rodríguez, Félix, and Linda Delgado. *Puerto Rican Women's*

History. New York: M.E. Sharpe, 1998.

McGregor, James. *The Lion and the Fox.* San Diego: Harcourt Brace Jovanovich Publishers, 1956.

McQuaid, Kim. "Corporate Liberalism in the American Business Community." *Business History Review* 52 (Autumn 1978): 342-368.

Mettler, Suzanne. *Dividing Citizens: Gender and Federalism in New Deal Public Policy.* Ithaca: Cornell University Press, 1998.

Muñoz Marín, Luis. *Memorias.* San Juan: Universidad Interamericana, 1982.

Naranjo, Consuelo, Miguel A. Puig Samper, and Luis Miguel Mora. *La Nación Soñada: Cuba, Puerto Rico y Filipinas ante el 98.* Madrid: Doce Calles, 1995.

Negrón de Montilla, Aida. *Americanization in Puerto Rico and the Public School System, 1900-1930.* Río Piedras: Puerto Rico Editorial Edil, 1970.

Ortíz, Altagracia. *Eighteenth Century Reforms in the Caribbean: Miguel de Muesas, Governor of Puerto Rico.* Rutherford, NJ: Fairleigh Dickinson University Press, 1983.

Osuna, José. *A History of Education in Puerto Rico.* New York: Arno Press, 1975.

Pabón, Carlos. "De Albizu a Madonna: para armar y desarmar la nacionalidad." *Bordes,* 1 (1995): 22-40.

Pagán, Bolívar. *Historia de los Partidos Políticos Puertorriqueños.* San Juan: Librería Campos, 1959.

Pantojas García, Emilio. "Desarrollismo y lucha de clases los límites del proyecto populista en Puerto Rico durante la década del 40." *Revista de Ciencias Sociales* 24 (Jul-Dec 1985): 355-390.

_____. Development Strategies. Boulder: Lynne Rienner Publishers, 1990.

Picó, Fernando. *Historia general de Puerto Rico.* Río Piedras: Editorial Huracán, 1986.

_____. *Cada guaraguao: galería de oficiales norteamericanos en Puerto Rico 1898- 1899.* Río Piedras: Ediciones Huracán, 1998.

Pigg, Stacey. "Constructing Social Categories through Place: Social Representation and Development in Nepal." *Comparative Studies in Society and History* 34 (1992): 491-513.

Quintero Rivera, Ángel. *Workers' Struggle in Puerto Rico: A Docu-*

mentary History. New York: Monthly Review Press, 1976.

———. *Conflictos de clase y política en Puerto Rico*. Río Piedras: Ediciones Huracán, 1986.

———. *Patricios y plebeyos: burgueses, hacendados, artesanos y obreros*. Río Piedras: Ediciones Huracán, 1988.

Radosh, Ronald, and Murray N. Rothbard. *A New History of Leviathan: Essays on the Rise of the American Corporate State*. New York: Dutton Publishers, 1972.

Raffuci, Carmen I. *El Gobierno Civil y la Ley Foraker*. Río Piedras: Editorial de la Universidad de Puerto Rico, 1981.

Raffuci, Carmen, Silvia Alvarez Curbelo, and Fernando Picó. *Senado de Puerto Rico: Ensayos de Historia Constitucional 1917-1992*. Río Piedras: Ediciones Huracán, 1992.

Rauch, Basil. *The History of the New Deal*. New York: Capricorn Books, 1963.

Rodríguez, Manuel R. "La reforma liberal en el contexto colonial: El Nuevo Trato y el Fair Labor Standard Act en Puerto Rico, 1938-1940." MA diss., University of Puerto Rico, 1996.

Roosevelt, Theodore. *Colonial Policies of the United States*. New York: Doubleday & Company, 1937.

Rosado, Marisa. *Las llamas de la aurora: un acercamiento a la biografía de Pedro Albizu Campos*. Santo Domingo: Editorial Corripio, 1991.

Rosario Natal, Carmelo. *La Juventud de Luis Muñoz Marín*. Río Piedras: Editorial Edil, 1989.

Said, Edward W. *Orientalism*. New York: Vintage Books, 1978.

Santana Rabell, Leonardo. *Planificación política un análisis crítico*. Río Piedras: Editorial Cultural, 1989.

Santiago-Valles, Kelvin. *Subject People and Colonial Discourses: Economic Transformation and Social Disorder in Puerto Rico, 1898-1947*. Albany: State University of New York Press, 1994.

Scarano, Francisco. "The Jíbaro Masquerade and the Subaltern Politics of Creole Identity Formation in Puerto Rico, 1745-1823." *American Historical Review* 101 (Dec. 1996): 1398-1431.

Schlesinger, Arthur M. *The Coming of the New Deal*. Boston: Houghton Mifflin Company, 1958.

Silva Gotay, Samuel. *Protestantismo y política en Puerto Rico 1898-*

1930. Río Piedras: Editorial de la Universidad de Puerto Rico, 1997.

Silvestrini, Blanca, and María Dolores Luque. *Los Trabajadores puertorriqueños y el Partido Socialista.* Río Piedras: Editorial de la Universidad de Puerto Rico, 1979.

⎯⎯⎯⎯. *Historia de Puerto Rico: trayectoria de un pueblo.* San Juan: Ediciones Cultural Panamericana, 1988.

Skalaroff, Rebecca Laureen. *Black Culture and the New Deal: The Quest for Civil Rights in the Roosevelt Era.* Chapel Hill: The University of North Carolina Press, 2009.

Solá, José O. "The Sugar Colonato of Puerto Rico: Social Transformation, Capitalism, and Competition in the Sugar Industry of Caguas." MA diss., University of South Carolina, 1995.

Taller de Formación Política. *Huelga en la caña, 1933-34.* Río Piedras: Ediciones Huracán, 1982.

⎯⎯⎯⎯. *No estamos pidiendo el cielo: Huelga Portuaria de 1938.* Río Piedras: Ediciones Huracán, 1988.

Tugwell, Rexford. *The Stricken Land.* New York: Doubleday and Company, 1947.

Villaronga, Gabriel. *Toward A Discourse of Consent: Mass Mobilization and Colonial Politics in Puerto Rico, 1932-1948.* Westport: Praeger, 2004.

www.ingramcontent.com/pod-product-compliance
Lightning Source LLC
Chambersburg PA
CBHW030234170426
43201CB00006B/219